CHAOS
and
The Plan

Why you should expect the unexpected

by
John M Legge

Chaos and the plan: Why you should expect the unexpected

This edition published by Information Strategy Planning Pty Ltd, Melbourne Australia.

ISBN-13: 978-1477504697
ISBN-10: 1477504699

First edition published by Schwarz and Wilkinson 1990 under the title "Chaos theory and business planning"

f

Contents

Contents   i

Introduction   iii

1. Models, Mathematics and Meaning   1

2. Deterministic Chaos   11

3. Roots and Branches   39

4. The Strange Levers of Power   53

5. The Map and the Markets   67

6. A New Look at Competition   87

7. The Hills and the Valleys   107

8. Taking Advantage   127

9. A Brief History of Chaology   141

10. Some Mathematics of Chaos   147

Introduction

IN 1990 MY LIFE had taken a new direction: after almost thirty years earning a living as a professional worker in the engineering and then the computer industries I decided to concentrate on teaching and writing. My first publisher asked me to write a book on chaos theory, a topic that had crept out of academia into the public consciousness, and I agreed.

I had been around long enough, as an executive involved in sales, marketing and business planning to learn the folly of relying on predictions. Possibilities: yes. Scenario planning: of course. At the end of every planning session, however, the only reliable prediction was that something that no-one had predicted would occur.

As a practising executive I had adapted to this fundamental uncertainty better than many of my colleagues, since I learnt from my childhood to be less surprised by predictive failure and less committed to the defence of theories that events disproved. Researching chaos theory for a book helped me realise that my cautious attitude had a strong mathematical and scientific basis: it was not a personality flaw.

There are many popular and professional books and magazines on management and planning, supplemented by many academic journals and conference reports. Most of these books and articles are focussed on pragmatic rules and case studies. While there is a considerable body of theory, the better and more consistent theories explain the past rather than providing guidance for the future. Most of the theories that purport to provide such guidance are neither consistent nor supported by my experience.

When I first came across the mathematics of chaos in Gleick's book[1] I felt that this was something which could begin to bring consistency to the theory of how a business in a market economy should plan. Chaos theory also provided a short cut refutation for many prescriptive theories that could otherwise have only been disproved by a process of painful trial and error.

The first fact to impress me about chaos is that deterministic chaos is a fact. It is not a visionary guess, but something that occurs and can be shown to occur in nature as well as in a computer. It is not something that can be adopted as a matter of choice, like heavy metal music or transcendental meditation.

Much business writing and education is crippled by being based upon the work of economists who think it proper to ignore chaotic reality in the attempt to put their discipline on a "scientific" basis. As I write this the world is caught up in a financial crisis with tens of millions of people out of work and many millions suffering serious privation. Australia is an island of relative prosperity in this global mess, saved from disaster by the apparently unlimited Chinese demand for raw materials.

My original book on chaos sold out a small edition and even appeared as an academic reference, but that seemed to be that. The onset of a global financial crisis in 2007 renewed my interest in chaos as a way of explaining how events that serious economists has assured us were impossible could still happen. Some friends and some members of my family urged me to revisit the topic, and this book is the result.

The current global financial crisis is being prolonged and deepened by political leaders taking advice from economists, who themselves base their recommendations on a set of theories collectively known as Dynamic Stochastic General Equilibrium, or DSGE.[2] DSGE has been used to make economic predictions and to guide economic policy for many years, and so its predictions can now be tested by examining facts.

One of the key predictions generated by DSGE is that financial crises such as the one under which the world is currently suffering can only occur once in a million years or so. Either the present generation is incredibly unlucky or DSGE theory has some serious flaws.

The economist defenders of DSGE blame external shocks or "black swan" events for the failure of their predictions; but chaos theory shows that they are wrong: reality is chaotic enough to cause extreme events far more frequently than DSGE can explain. The truly great economist Joseph Schumpeter coined the term "Ricardian vice" to describe the work of economists who build their conclusions into their assumptions, and DSGE is riddled with it.

Economic chaos is not restricted to the global economy. Writers in the business press regularly praise the entrepreneurial acumen of managers who achieved high profits and higher growth rates by their superior vision and market insights. Less kind things tend to be said later amidst the debris left by their collapsed empires, but few writers can claim to have forecasted these collapses until they were imminent, and not always then.

Caution is not an adequate basis for success either. In hard times, as in 1990–91, 1997–98 and in the years after the onset of the Global Financial Crisis in 2007 many conservatively managed small and medium businesses were forced into receivership. As with the paper entrepreneurs, the mistakes these business's managers made are glaringly obvious — in hindsight. Banks have destroyed many apparently prosperous small and medium businesses by withdrawing credit: credit which had been freely granted earlier, and where nothing the business itself has done can explain the change in the banks' policy. Such businesses are victims of chaos, not in their own business or in their markets, but in the banks' lending policies.

The pattern of excessively easy credit, followed by an arbitrary raising of interest rates and withdrawal of credit facilities, is a typical chaotic phenomenon because within the banks, information and policy flows are out of phase and *stay* out of phase. The only way that they detect an error in their policies is when they overshoot their policy targets: too many non-performing loans at one end of the scale, and too few customers of any kind at the other.

This book has been written to be intelligible to people with even less grasp of mathematics than I have. I have put a brief summary of some of the salient points of chaos theory into Chapter 10. The mathematics-averse need not try to read it, while serious mathematicians will go straight to the more serious literature.

This book is my original work, but most of the ideas in it are the work of others. I have attempted to acknowledge my sources in the endnotes; to anyone whose contribution I have failed to acknowledge, I offer my sincere apologies. I hope that readers will find the book stimulating and amusing. Those that are looking for detailed answers to their problems will, I fear, be disappointed. The great lesson of chaos theory is that every situation is different and every problem is unique. There are no infallible rules.

John M Legge
August 2012

Endnotes

1   Gleick, James (1987), *Chaos: making a new science*, London: Heinemann.

2   Quiggin, J (2010), *Zombie Economics: How dead ideas still walk among us*, Princeton NJ: Princeton University Press.

1. Models, Mathematics and Meaning

The role of the model

HUMANS ARE CREATIVE beings. Men and women are continually creating new things, or bringing about a new state of things. Occasionally this creativity finds a dramatic expression, as when Einstein created the Theory of Relativity. Most acts of creation are less dramatic than that, yet few people go through a day without doing something or having some idea that has not been done or thought before.

The idea precedes the action. Apart from a few learned or instinctive responses, people think about the effects of what they are proposing to do before they do it. Sometimes they are wrong. Children and particularly creative adults frequently achieve effects that neither they nor anyone else expected. The sequence thought, action, observation is how humans work and learn. Thoughts, once had, are transferred by speech and writing to other humans, where they become in time an influence on the behaviour pattern of the entire human race.

This is, suggests Richard Dawkins[1], humankind's key evolutionary advantage. A naked man would appear to be a pleasant and easy meal for a tiger, lion or wolf. Yet lions, tigers and wolves live on human sufferance in zoos and nature reserves, while humans dominate the planet. Plans and tools triumphed over tooth and claw. The stick and the cliff became the spear and the trap. Always the flow is from the accidental to the transformed, from the simple to the elaborate. At every stage the early object becomes part of the model for the more developed one. First comes the model, then the idea, then the prototype of a new generation of manufactured objects.

For relatively small-scale projects, like cooking dinner or writing a sales proposal, the person charged with the task of creating a new, functional product may move directly from the raw materials to the finished article. For larger and more elaborate projects, the people carrying them out complete them in a number of steps. A common intermediate step is to construct a model of the desired final result. The model may be wholly abstract or it may be a full size replica, or anything in between.

Somebody planning to build a new house buys or copies a plan. Someone preparing an ambitious meal consults a recipe book and then writes out a menu. An architect, trying to explain a concept to a client, may arrange to have a scale model constructed. The plans, and the recipe book, are models, but abstract ones. The model building, made out of balsa wood and Perspex, is really an abstract model but it *looks* more realistic than a paper plan or an architectural rendering. This makes it somehow more convincing and easier to understand. In every case, the model reduces the risks involved in the full-scale project. It increases the understanding of the project, both for the constructor and for the planned users, and makes it more likely that the users will get what they really want.

Models get a lot of use in industry. The designers of a new car make scale and eventually full size models in order to refine the styling. Designers of a new aircraft build scale models and subject them to intensive testing in wind tunnels to test the drag coefficient and establish its aerodynamic parameters. Creating and testing such models are expensive and time consuming activities; but still far less expensive than setting up and then abandoning a full scale production system.

The designers of a new class of boat rely on models to test sailing and stability characteristics for various possible hull shapes. In most cases the person using a model knows that the full size prototype will not look or behave *exactly* like the model, but the model gives valuable information that would have cost more and taken longer to get another way. If the model boat is stable, this does not guarantee that the prototype will be stable, but suggests that it might be. If a model boat capsizes instantly when it is put in the water, this suggests that this particular model is a poor basis for a future full-scale design.

The fundamental justification for the effort spent on building and testing models before constructing full size prototypes and commencing production is not a lack of knowledge or a weakness in our mathematical tools: it is because the ultimate products will enter a complex environment where chaos is omnipresent.

The styling of a new model of motor car cannot be developed from first principles because prospective buyers do not merely consider their own impression of a car: they wonder what their friends, neighbours and colleagues will think of their choice. While some of these friends, neighbours and colleagues will be severe individualists immune to the opinion of others, most will also be concerned with the general opinion as well as their own. To paraphrase JM Keynes, the most favoured style will not be the one that a typical person thinks the most attractive, or even what the average person thinks the most attractive, but what the typical person believes that the average person believes to be the most attractive: it is an infinite regress.

Unlike mass market products like motor cars, ships and aircraft are chosen by technical experts, and average opinion doesn't enter into it; but their performance in reality remains an incomputable problem because of chaos: turbulence in this instance. Designing a boat to sail on perfectly calm waters or an aircraft to navigate cloudless and windless skies would present few challenges to an experienced naval architect or aeronautical engineer. Boats on real seas and aircraft in real skies, encounter turbulence, a truly chaotic phenomenon any instance of which is unlikely to be repeated in the life of the universe.

With no over-arching formula to follow, and with a complete study of all the possible operating circumstances beyond the reach of the most powerful computer, naval architects and aeronautical engineers test their model in the most extreme circumstances that they can reproduce and hope that their boat or aeroplane will never encounter anything more severe. They are not always successful.

Models play an important part in the development of children. Most toys are models of objects from the adult world, but models where the child can play at participating in the real world without risking real world consequences. Toy cars crash without causing insurance problems. Toy people are left in the rain overnight without provoking a visit from the child welfare officer.

None of this is new: the use of models and pictures is as old as humanity. For many anthropologists, the use of models and pictures *defines* humanity. Since the seventeenth century, and even more strongly since 1950, mankind has become familiar with two new kinds of models of reality. These are the use of mathematics in the physical sciences, and the use of mathematical models and computer simulations in business and government.

Mathematics goes back long before the seventeenth century, but it was not until Sir Isaac Newton's work that men began to see that the physical world could be explained in terms of mathematical laws. Before Newton, and going back to Pythagoras and Plato[2] mathematics had been seen as an abstract discipline by which men could begin to understand the Gods. Mathematical laws were held to prove something about God's rules for human conduct, for example. Mathematics was not believed to be relevant to navigation, or useful for building a house, at least by the classical Greeks.

de Moivre's theorem

The mathematician de Moivre discovered an elegant and concise relationship between e, the base of natural logarithms, π, the ratio of the circumference of a circle to its diameter, and i, the square root of minus one. It is:

$$e^{i\pi} + 1 = 0$$

Mathematicians find this a wondrous thing. Non-mathematicians find it boring.

Mathematical models

Sir Isaac Newton showed that mathematical formulae could have two interpretations. On the one hand, a formula is an abstract statement about the relationship between different logical statements. On the other hand, a mathematical expression frequently provides a model of some aspect of the real universe. A short formula can predict the time of rising of Mars from any point on Earth for thousands of years into the future. A similar and even shorter formula can describe the path of a rock falling from a cliff.

Both these formulae reflect Newton's "law" of gravity. It is important to remember two things. Firstly, Mars and the rock were there before Newton discovered his law. Secondly, there is no transcendental police force enforcing the law of gravity: a rock does not fall in a parabola for fear of being fined, or having its falling licence suspended.

Newton's law is a simple formula from which a mathematician, an astronomer or a physicist can build a mathematical model which will provide an *approximate* description of a falling rock, or of the orbit of Mars as seen from a particular point on Earth. Sometimes this relationship is reversed. Occasionally people talk as if the proper behaviour for a rock is to fall in a perfect parabola, and the various things that divert it from this course are unfortunate temporal accidents. This way of thinking can be traced directly to Plato.

A practical person, a mountaineer or a quarry master, knows that a real rock does not fall in a perfect parabola. It is slowed by air resistance, diverted by gusts of wind, bounced off outlying ledges and brushed by vegetation. The air, the wind, the ledges, and the trees are real: the formula is the abstract concept. The model is simple and easy to understand; reality is complex and messy.

The classic Greek philosopher Plato would have been perfectly at home in a debate about quantum physics. Most quantum physicists hold that perceived reality is merely the "condensation" of a wave equation. In quantum mechanical theory, something that is not being observed only exists as an abstract potential. Laymen can study the Controversy of Schrödinger's Cat in order to get a flavour of the debate. They can rest assured that quantum physics has no relevance whatever to their normal worldly conduct, except in their dealings with quantum physicists.

Familiarity with mathematical models sometimes introduces a particular type of practical error. A mathematical formula has an exact result. Most people who use mathematical models will be aware that the real world result will probably differ from the exact mathematical one. They may severely under-estimate the magnitude of the variation. If the computer says that the answer is forty-two, then the user might assume that the practical result will be something like forty-two: between thirty-eight and forty-six, for example. Sometimes this is true, but far more often than was once believed, it is not.

Plato's cave

Plato used the metaphor of the cave to explain his view of the difference between human perception and reality. Plato asked his listeners to consider men sitting in a cave with their back to the entrance, observing the shadows cast on the back wall of the cave as other men, gods and animals passed between the entrance to the cave and the sun.

To Plato, reality was perfect, symmetrical and immutable, and it was only our human limitations that prevented us from understanding it. Plato placed considerable emphasis on mathematics, since he believed that geometric construction and proof allowed humans to approach divine understanding of reality "outside the cave".

Modern mathematics has turned Plato's metaphor on its head. It is our perceptions, including our mathematical formulae and logical demonstrations, which are built from an idealised model of the world: reality is more chaotic and unpredictable than anything Plato ever imagined as the human lot.

Robots and computers

The classical economist and Scottish moralist Adam Smith[3] thought that industrial workers were quasi morons, endlessly performing a few easily learned tasks. Many people who have never been inside a modern factory imagine that nothing has changed since Smith wrote. In fact, human workers are now too expensive and too inaccurate to be used for repetitive tasks. In a modern factory, simple repetitive tasks are delegated to robots and programmed machines. Humans are engaged to maintain and program the machines and to carry out those tasks too complex to be programmed. A modern Japanese car factory requires human labour for about eleven hours per car, while robots and programmed machines perform the equivalent of a hundred and fifty hours of human labour.

Charles Dickens and others described the dreadful life of a clerk in a Victorian office. Life for such clerks involved long hours at a standing desk, adding endless columns of numbers or transcribing long boring letters under the eye of a sarcastic superior. Their pitiful pay was barely adequate to pay for the laundering of their precious white collars. The modern clerk does not spend his or her day adding endless columns of figures. The modern office uses computers that are programmed to carry out the repetitive work. The computers produce exception reports for those transactions that require human judgement for their proper completion.

The robot and the computer have added greatly to the sum of human happiness by taking over the boring and the repetitive elements of modern work. It was once feared that automation would lead to increased unemployment. In practice, the demand by humans for humans to carry out value adding activities has proved to be effectively unlimited. Computers and robotics have added to human happiness in another way. Very lively electronic games have been created, which fully engage the imagination of the players and give them considerable pleasure. The pleasure is such that some players clearly prefer the game world to the real one.

Whether, like quantum physicists, electronic game players believe that the game (or model) world is the true reality, while what the commoners call reality is the approximation, is not certain but is a little improbable. After all, the game player must enter the real world for long enough to get the money that feeds the machines in the arcades, buys copies of the latest games or keeps the Internet connection open.

Another aspect of the use of modern technology to create models has had a much more equivocal impact. The computer, and most notably the personal computer spreadsheet, has enabled many more people to build mathematical models, and has enabled these models to produce a far greater volume of output than manual methods could ever have achieved. The modern spreadsheet program is an immensely powerful business tool, and few people would consider planning a new product or trying to manage a significant business without making extensive use of a spreadsheet program such as Excel™ and its open source variants. Spreadsheets can be used to keep track of reality and to make forecasts of the financial and other effects of various contingencies and management choices. Trouble starts when a spreadsheet user becomes an addict, and begins to believe that changing some of the numbers on the spreadsheet is sufficient to cause an equivalent change in the real world.

As long as spreadsheet addicts merely stare at columns of numbers and at the various kinds of graphs that the better packages produce, no great harm is done. Spreadsheet addicts whose influence is confined to a single business can do no worse than damage that business, and in any case their results are likely to be moderated by the common sense of the business's other executives.

Unfortunately, the use of mathematical models has spread to two classes of people with a significant influence upon public policy. On the one hand, there are green extremists. On the other, there are the mainstream economists. Both of these groups exhibit an uncritical fondness for mathematical models, combined with an excessively linear mode of reasoning. They then use the results of these models and linear arguments uncritically. Like theoretical physicists, "they are often in error but never in doubt". In debate, and when advising on public policy, extreme economists and extreme green activists refer almost exclusively to their model results. The real world is ignored entirely or selectively trawled for numbers that support the model answer.

The purest mathematical economists express themselves in partial differential equations. Such equations are easy to write but infernally difficult to solve: mathematicians have demonstrated that, for every soluble set of differential equations, there is an infinite number of insoluble sets. There are two ways past this roadblock. One is to make enough simplifying assumptions to reduce any problem to a soluble set of equations, which is harmless until the economist who does this announces his conclusions as facts without restating the simplifying or counterfactual assumptions necessary to reaching them. (Today's economists are quick to accuse each other of Ricardian vice, but most of them are slow to recognise it in themselves.)

The very useful spreadsheet

A large English company believed in planning, by which they meant the production of pro forma profit and loss statements for several years into the future.

They also believed that a successful strategy could be summarised in a few simple numerical rules, and the duties of senior managers consisted of stating and revising these rules. The senior business planner grew prematurely aged in the task of preparing endless revised forecasts, each being rendered obsolete by the next revelation to strike his superiors. The aging process was arrested and reversed by the arrival of the personal computer and spreadsheet. Now the senior planner could produce forecasts two or three times per day, confident that each accurately reproduced the latest management fad.

For a few months the company had a chief executive who asked questions rather than spouted formulae, and the planner was devastated. Soon that manager was moved on, and the old order restored. None of the plans ever bore any relationship to ultimate reality, but that was never the point of producing them.

The other route is to use a computer to solve the original set of equations.

While there is nothing intrinsically wrong with the use of a competently prepared computer model, the process conceals some major traps. A computer model is simultaneously the statement of, and a means of solution to, a set of complex mathematical equations[4]. These equations are probably approximations to another set of complex equations which in turn were developed empirically or theoretically after observing reality, or reading some earlier worker's account of her observations.

Professional mathematicians and engineers approach the solution of systems of such equations with profound caution. The results of research into chaos theory over the past thirty years have added immeasurably to this caution: even if the labour of attempting to solve the system of equations is rewarded by a solution, chaos may render the results valueless except in the very short term. Critics of the various extreme factions among economists and in the ecology movement can and do challenge the assumptions that are used to develop their various models. Relatively few such critics have yet picked up the point that the entire process from assumptions to conclusions may be invalid: even if the assumptions are valid, and the data reasonably accurate, the results can still be totally unreliable.

Much of this book is about the consequences of this difference between the number predicted by a mathematical model and the number likely to be discovered in a real world experiment. We describe the application of the results of chaos research to basic economics and the consequences for business planning.

Endnotes

---

[1] Richard Dawkins (1989), *The Selfish Gene*, Oxford: Oxford University Press..

[2] Pythagoras was a semi-mythical figure of the sixth century BC, while Plato flourished at the beginning of the fourth century BC. The Pythagoreans and the Platonists showed a keen interest in abstract mathematics, but deprecated any attempt to find a practical use for their work. Kepler, who discovered that the planets moved in elliptical orbits in the seventeenth century AD, started out trying to show that the planetary orbits bore some relationship to Platonic geometry.

[3] Adam Smith (1723-1790): a Scottish philosopher and moralist whose book *The Wealth of Nations* (Glasgow: 1776 and many subsequent editions) is the foundation economics text. Smith advocated the substantial deregulation of commerce and industry (but not finance). His name has, rather unjustly, become a rallying cry for the New Right.

[4] Note for the vaguely mathematical: A spreadsheet almost inevitably forms a set of partial *difference* equations, while most mathematical models are developed a partial *differential* equations. The differential equations are approximations to the behaviour of a world of discrete objects, which should properly be described by a different set of difference equations. The fact that the best scientific research is at three removes from the model should be a warning of possible trouble with the results. The process is likely to conceal true chaos and introduce false chaos as well.

2. Deterministic Chaos

Chaos in the world

THE WORLD IS a turbulent place, where the most certain things about tomorrow are surprise and confusion. However people have won their living, chaos has lurked at every turn. The primitive hunter stalking a wild sheep tripped over a tiger. The early farmer lost the crop to hail or to elephants, while inexplicable diseases ravaged the herds and flocks. The early trader was surprised by bandits, or caught in a storm at sea, or stuck on the track in a blizzard with a foundered horse.

The modern businessperson and farmer face these hazards in thinly disguised forms, with one or two new ones special to our age. Hail and wild animals still threaten farmers, and now they must face a new hurdle. When they have thwarted the insects, frustrated the birds, scared the elephants or kangaroos, dodged the hail, negotiated with the contractor and secured their harvest they must still sell it. Farmers do not know until their cheques are in the bank whether the sale of their crops will pay the costs of growing and harvesting them, and still leave a margin to support their families and mortgage payments. Modern financial markets allow many farmers to experience these problems in reverse: they can sell their crop on the futures market, which gives them the money that they need to live on, but they then face the risk that hail, fire, elephants or kangaroos will damage or destroy their crop, leaving them with an enforceable delivery contract and nothing to deliver.

The managers of most businesses do not expect trouble from kangaroos and elephants, but they are not free of problems. If one container in a hundred spends six months on a six-week journey, it will be the one carrying a vital shipment to the business's most valued customer. When the business's supplies are in the warehouse the managers do not know whether there will be any customers to buy them. If there are customers in droves, the managers do not know whether the wholesalers and retailers will take all the profit and then some, leaving the business to survive on the whim of its bankers.

For as long as people have been able to write, they have written about chaos and thought and written about possible explanations of chaos and ways to cope with it. Some of these explanations are poetic, and some are religious. Some religions teach us to accept chaos as a proof of God's love for us. Others suggest that we should withdraw from this chaotic world by meditation and self-denial. For most of

Chaos in government

In the 1950s the Australian Government decided that the Commonwealth Scientific and Industrial Research Organisation (CSIRO) would be funded for two major research programmes rather than the three that it had commenced.

Australians had invented radio astronomy, they had achieved world leadership in some important aspects of computer development and they had produced some interesting results from rain making experiments. The Australian Government sought advice in the matter from the English Government, and the English Government sent out an expert seconded from one of the English business equipment companies.

The expert advised that Australia's proper function was to supply raw materials, principally wool, for British factories, and successful rainmaking would assist this process. Computers could be built by anyone. The Australian Government accepted this advice and cancelled the computer research program.

Thirty years later computers, developed in other countries, were used to develop the theory of deterministic chaos. As a corollary of this research it was demonstrated that directed weather modification, such as rain making, was a wholly futile exercise. The Australian rain making experiments were abandoned.

human history, mathematicians have admired and worked on the smooth, the round, the predictable, and the regular. A complete class of mathematics was called "pure maths" because it was thought to have had no relationship to the real world at all.

In this century, and more strongly in the last twenty-five years, many mathematicians have developed an interest in the rough, the unpredictable, and the irregular. They have given this study a name, or a number of names. Some call it Chaology: others call it Non-Linear Dynamics, or Dynamic Systems Theory. To many, chaos studies are just a part of the broader field of Complexity Theory.

So what?

Most businessmen and marketeers have known about chaos for a long time, since they live in the middle of it. It may be reassuring to know that mathematicians and physicists now agree that yes, real life is chaotic, and no, your problems are not imaginary. Why should a practical man or woman be interested in the fact that mathematicians have discovered chaos? The reason is that a new theory gives us a new way of looking at things, and this may suggest new solutions to old problems.

Yes, the urgent container may travel from Melbourne to Sydney via Cape Town, Amsterdam, Omsk and New York, but *no*, this is not a proof that someone is trying to get at you, just that chaos discovered a flaw in the control system for some or all of the transport route.

Yes, the bloke down the road may be doing better than you at the same business in spite of being a poor workman and a slob, but *no* there is no magic secret ingredient: chaos has made him lucky and you are going to have to work hard to catch up.

Yes, your firm has wound up on top of a new market in spite of the technical experts telling you that your product was inferior, and *yes* the experts could well have been right. You have been lucky to get on top: you are going to have to work hard to stay there.

Chaos theory has shown many important things, among them:

- a great deal of very useful information about a complex system such as a market or an economy can be derived from a small number of manageable equations,
- studying these equations has given mathematicians and others a whole set of new insights into the limits of predictability in the behaviour of complex systems.

Chapter 10 discusses these issues in slightly greater depth.

A new state of nature

This book has very little mathematics in it, and most of that is in the last chapters. The non-mathematical reader is urged to plough through the next couple of pages, because the words introduced in them are really needed to understand the rest of the book.

Before chaos theory arrived, mathematicians and engineers thought that systems could be in one of three states. A system could be *stable*, or in its *ground state*. A system consisting of a heap of bricks on the ground is stable, and not very interesting. All real systems will eventually fall into their ground state unless they are continually supplied with energy. A system could be *oscillating*, like the pendulum of a grandfather clock or the string of a violin being bowed. The necessary energy to keep the pendulum swinging comes from the springs or weights in the clock. The energy to keep the string sounding comes from the violinist's arm.

A smoothly flowing system such as water in an irrigation channel is a special case of oscillation, with a zero fundamental frequency. The energy to drive the flow in the irrigation channel comes from gravity, to pull the water down, and the sun, to drive the weather system that puts fresh water into the catchments. Dams and flood control systems smooth out the unpredictable rainfall and provide a steady source of water. A zero fundamental frequency state is sometimes called a *steady state*, which distinguishes it from the stable state. In conversation, the terms *stable* and *steady* are sometime used interchangeably, as in *stable flow*. The context usually makes it clear which state is meant.

Scientists were aware that some behaviour seemed extremely complex, notably turbulent flow in fluids. The best description of turbulence before the application of chaos theory to the problem saw it as an extremely complicated pattern of oscillations.

The third state a system could be in was *exploding*, when the driving energy of the system causes oscillations or other reactions that build to a crescendo that destroys the system itself. An apocryphal story about the great tenor Caruso described a party trick, which illustrated this point. He was supposed to have taken a crystal wine glass and rubbed it to determine its characteristic note, and then sung this precise note *fortissimo* until the glass shattered. Laboratory studies have confirmed that it is possible to use tuned sound to shatter a wine glass, but suggest that the energy required is beyond any human singer.

Chaos, or more accurately *deterministic chaos*, is the system state between oscillating and exploding. Turbulent flow in fluids is now seen to be a special case of chaos. Systems in a chaotic state are not stable, because they are continually changing. They are not oscillating, or if it is the pattern is so complicated that it cannot be detected. A real life chaotic system may never repeat itself within the lifetime of the universe.

A chaotic system is not exploding: a cloud is perpetually changing, but it stays a cloud. Most realistic systems can be in any one of these four states depending on the external conditions, including the available energy levels. Sometimes a system can be caught in one state until some shock triggers a change into the expected state for the conditions. An old TV set that hisses and fizzes chaotically, may, if banged in the correct way, flip into a state in which a picture is visible.

Imagine a stack of bricks on the back of a truck that is being driven on a rough road. Initially the truck is travelling slowly. It hits an occasional big bump, causing the bricks to jump, but they settle down again. The system of bricks is in a stable state. If the driver presses the accelerator and increases the level of energy being applied the truck will travel faster. The stack of bricks will begin to rock from side to side and forward and backward. This is the oscillatory state. If the driver continues to press the accelerator and the truck goes faster still, the stack of bricks will collapse into a heap. Each bump and shake will shoot bricks into the air. Every time they land it is in a new pattern. The system is now in a *chaotic* state. Finally the truck could reach such a speed that the bumps become so severe that bricks begin to bounce right out of the truck onto the road. The system has become explosive: unless the truck slows down all the bricks will vanish and the system will finally achieve stability through annihilation.

A stack of bricks provides one example of a relatively complex system. The weather provides another, and one of great economic importance. As far as can be worked out, chaotic weather is just what we need. The only wholly predictable weather pattern would resemble winter at the South Pole, with the whole world covered with snow and ice, and a few slowly moving icy breezes. Stable weather is only found on dead planets circling lifeless suns.

The trigger for Chaos

Chaos is a state where accurate long-term prediction is impossible.

For a business, this can mean that it has been operating for months or years according to proven principles when a hole appears in the figures, apparently "out of the blue". For no apparent reason a regular customer simply doesn't place his normal monthly order, or a regular supplier puts the business on a 50% ration.

Sometimes this catastrophe follows from a clear, large cause. The supplier may have been hit by a strike, or the customer's store may have been struck by lightning and burnt down. Depending upon where the boundaries of the system are drawn, such large events could be considered as arising within the system or being random strokes of fate coming from outside it. Of the two examples used here, an industrial relations problem could usually be described as having its origins within the system, while lightning is generally classified as an "act of God", and assumed to come from outside.

Chaos can be provoked by no sudden cause at all. Suppose that the major customer has been placing a regular order for a hundred units, because that is where the next discount step cuts in, but only using an average of 90 units per month. This sort of thing can go on for years. One day a keen-eyed accountant spots the build up of stock and orders the orders for the next three months to be cancelled. Someone who had the time to find out all the facts about this particular supplier-customer relationship could confidently predict that *eventually* the over-stocking would be noticed. Predicting *exactly* when, or even in which year, the customer would hire an eager beaver into the accounts department, and how long it would take the new accountant to start looking in the warehouse, is beyond any reasonable human capability.

It is in the nature of complex systems that such situations develop silently and unobserved until some apparently trivial event causes a major change. This major change will have repercussions right through the system, and there is no certainty that the system will ever settle down into a predictable pattern of behaviour again. In the example just discussed, there were just two quantities involved, the rate of consumption and the rate of ordering. Both were being managed according to quite consistent rules. Between them they created the precursor for chaos. In a real life business there will be hundreds of variables to manage and millions of opportunities for time bombs to begin developing.

Chaos is normal. It is stability and predictability that is unnatural—or a sign of impending doom and destruction.

The Gaia hypothesis

The weather on earth has changed a lot over geological as well as historical time, but never by quite as much as most scientists would have expected.

James Lovelock proposed the Gaia hypothesis. He suggested that some life forms have evolved to act in ways that tend to limit the swings in the system. If the weather gets too hot, they stimulate cloud formation, for example, which causes more sunlight to reflect.

The hypothesis proposes that the entire biosphere should be regarded as a single, self-regulating adaptive system. We now know that such systems don't come to a steady state but rather, on a timescale of tens or hundreds of thousands of years, swing between hot and cold periods—as the geological record shows that the Earth has done.

The seeds of Chaos

The starting point of chaos is usually called feedback, but it is really feed forward. What is done to the system *now* will affect the way the system behaves at some time in the future. Often timing is critical. For many systems, something can be done at a given time, and after waiting for some further time the system will "forget" what the first stimulus was and react quite independently to the second one.

Such systems may respond chaotically under repeated rapid stimuli and oscillate or settle down to a steady state when the rate of arrival of the stimuli is slower. Consider the domestic shower, or at least, the old fashioned type controlled by a hot and a cold tap. When both taps are turned on, the shower will probably be too hot or too cold. If the person in the shower tries to cool down an excessively hot shower by turning the cold tap on further, there will be no immediate effect because the water takes a finite time to travel along the pipes between the taps and the shower head. If the person becomes impatient and turns the tap further still the shower will suddenly swing from too hot to too cold. If the person then repeats the same process in reverse, the shower is likely to swing back to too hot.

Only when a person taking a shower makes a small adjustment and waits for the temperature to settle down before making another one can they be sure of getting the temperature "just right". Studies of the artificial stock market maintained by the Santa Fé Institute suggest that the same effect is at work in real stock markets. If buyers assembled a portfolio and waited a year or two to see how the firms in which they had shares performed before considering buying or selling any shares, the stock market would be a quiet place with few trades and no sudden changes in price. People in real stock exchanges buy and sell shares after holding them for minutes, and the relationship between the relative prices of shares and the relative performances of companies is at best imprecise.[1]

Steering a big ship can easily degenerate into slow motion but potentially fatal chaos if the helmsman is inexperienced or incompetent. When the rudder is first pulled over the stern is pushed off the line of the ship's course and the ship starts to turn around a vertical axis. If the helm is just set to straight ahead once the boat has come around to the desired new heading the ship will continue to turn; slowly, but because of the weight and length of a ship, with considerable force. The inexperienced helmsman may then over-correct in the other direction sending the ship on a slow motion but wild zigzag course until an experienced boatswain takes charge or the ship hits something solid.

A hallmark of chaos is *sensitivity to initial conditions*. When a system is operating in a chaotic state a very small change to a stimulus can have an arbitrarily large effect on the state of the system at some later time. Deterministic chaos means that knowing a great deal about a system does not allow one to forecast its long-range behaviour accurately. It does not necessarily mean that anything is going whiz or hiss. A game of snooker is chaotic: no player, even a world champion, could play an identical game twice in succession with every ball going into the same pocket in the same order after the same number of strokes.

The weather and the greenhouse effect

Exactly why the weather on Earth has never collapsed into a steady icy state or exploded in thermal runaway like Venus is not clear to meteor-ologists. The Gaia hypothesis provides an attractive systems theory alternative: it suggests that life forms are a part of the feedback loop that controls and stabilises the global weather system.

Life on earth as we know it depends on the availability of liquid water: at Earth's atmospheric pressure this means that average temper-atures must be between $0°$ and $100°$ Celsius ($273°$ and $373°$ Kelvin, or Absolute). If Earth's atmosphere was transparent to infra red (heat) radiation the average temperature would be about $278°$ Kelvin or $8°$ Celsius: ice caps would cover much of the Earth.

While some of the gases in the Earth's atmosphere are transparent to infra red radiation some, notably water and carbon dioxide (CO_2) are not, and these gases provide a blanket letting high energy radiation through to warm the Earth and preventing lower energy radiation escaping to cool it.

A few hundred million years ago the Earth's atmosphere contained much more CO_2 than it does today, and average temperatures were much higher. The evolution of plants, which absorb CO_2 from the atmosphere and add water to create carbohydrates and in the process releasing oxygen reduced CO_2 levels and raised oxygen levels; this reduced the effectiveness of the greenhouse "blanket" and the Earth cooled. The cooler Earth and the reduced availability of CO_2 slowed plant metabolism and the temperature stopped falling.

Plants are not the only life form on Earth. Animals eat plants and metabolise their carbohydrates with the aid of atmospheric oxygen, releasing CO_2 in the process and so increasing the effectiveness of the greenhouse blanket and tending to warm the Earth. If animals get too successful the amount of active plant matter on Earth falls, the CO_2 level rises, raising the temperature with it; and while animal life will be restricted by the lack of food plant growth will be encouraged by higher temperatures and more available CO_2.

Evolutionary pressures on both plants and animals prevent any stable equilibrium developing: there have been extended hot and cold periods. In coarse terms average temperatures have been kept above freezing for many million years; possibly the whole period of life on the Earth.

There are other feedback loops operating: if the earth cools the polar ice sheets expand; ice reflects more heat than water so the Earth will cool further; but when water freezes the dissolved CO_2 is released to the atmosphere, increasing the effectiveness of the greenhouse blanket and causing average temperatures to rise.

Climatic conditions on Earth are subject to many conflicting forces, and the result is not a single stable average temperature but rather a chaotic temperature pattern: deterministic in that every change is explicable in hindsight but chaotic because the future trajectory is impossible to forecast.

Anthropogenic climate change

Humans, as animal products of evolution, reproduce as vigorously as the environment will permit; more, because of successful industrialisation, humans have largely evaded the pressures that restricted the development of former top predators. We have cleared the forest for agriculture, restricted genetic diversity in order to maximise the productivity of our chosen food species; and released vast amounts of CO_2 by extracting and burning fossil fuels. In the traditional struggle between plants, which tend to cool the Earth, and animals, which tend to warm it, we have turbocharged the animals.

If all human activity ceased at some point in the next few hundred years, the natural stabilisers would reverse the present effects of global warming, though not overnight: in the past the swing from warming to cooling and vice versa has typically taken many thousands of years. What is unprecedented is the speed with which human activity has altered the atmosphere, raising the CO_2 concentration by 30 per cent or so in just over two hundred years.

James Lovelock, the author of the Gaia Hypothesis, is extremely worried about this assault on the natural temperature system and as long ago as 1994 he predicted that a "business as usual" scenario would lead to planetary disaster.[2] Having been raised to demigod status by the environmental movement, Lovelock shocked them by calling for an urgent program to replace coal fired power stations with nuclear powered ones, as the only way to avoid planetary warming of 5° to 8° and rendering much of the planet uninhabitable by humans.[3]

For observers with the luxury of living for a million or more years the climate of Earth over the next half a million or so years could give an interesting example of what happens to a complex system when it is suddenly forced a long way from its usual trajectory. Lovelock suggested that the climate might take a hundred thousand years to recover; some other writers have suggested that a reversal of warming could occur much sooner than that with an equally vicious swing in the other direction. Even if humans do nothing explicit about climate change, rising sea levels as the ice caps melt and other nasty effects will put an end to most industrial activity allowing the return of the plants, increased CO_2 absorption, and falling temperatures.

There is no reason to suppose that this reversal will stop at a point where the Earth is again a pleasant place for humans to live and every reason to expect a violent overshoot, hence the return of the ice ages.

The fundamental lesson is that the Earth's climate is a truly chaotic system, one in which short term behaviour may be predicted with some accuracy as in the weather forecast but medium and long term prediction is impossible. The assumption that things will "turn out right" if we go on adding CO_2 is exceptionally improbable and those who advocate "business as usual" are fools or rogues.

Phase diagrams

Most people are familiar with maps of one sort or another. One of the uses of a map is that it lets you see that some routes will not work; another is that it can serve as a record of a journey. A street map is usually adequate for navigating around a town, and it will usually be used descriptively: "We will drive North up Smith Street to Princes Street, then turn left..." and in the past tense, with or without a pencil, we can describe a journey the same way. Aircraft and ships do not usually rely on street directories, and express their intentions and their history in terms of waypoints and bearings.

Whether we are talking of a navigator's chart or a driver's street directory there is a fairly straightforward correspondence between the picture on the sheet or page and the ground or ocean that will be

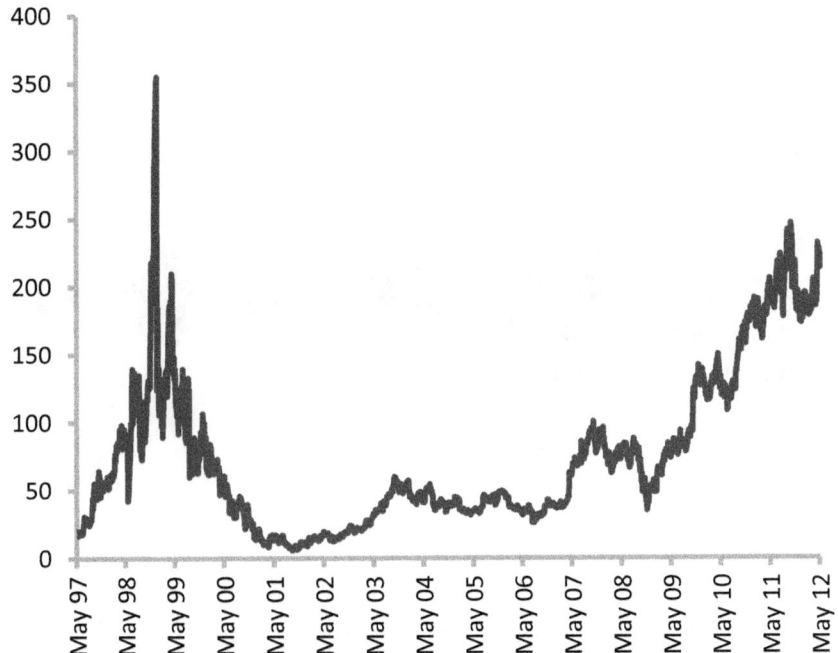

Figure 2.1   Daily closing share prices

Amazon.com Inc's daily closing share price from the firm's first listing until
early 2012 (adjusted for splits). Source: Yahoo.com

traversed. Maps and charts often express this by stating the scale to
which they are produced: a 1:100 000 scale means that one centimetre on
the map represents one kilometres of reality, for example.   Phase
diagrams are charts without a direct geographic analogue.

Figure 2.1 is a chart recording the price of a fairly volatile US
stock. Moving from right to left on the chart has nothing to do with
travelling east; it means that we are looking at later days. Similarly,
moving up the chart does not mean that we are travelling north, but that
we are looking at higher prices. The line on this chart records an
abstract journey: how some speculators thought that other speculators
thought that other speculators thought that the Amazon.com share price
was going to move.

An alternative view of Amazon's share price (Figure 2.2) period
shows how much it has changed in successive daily periods, rising or
falling by over 20 per cent in a single day. The "official" economist's

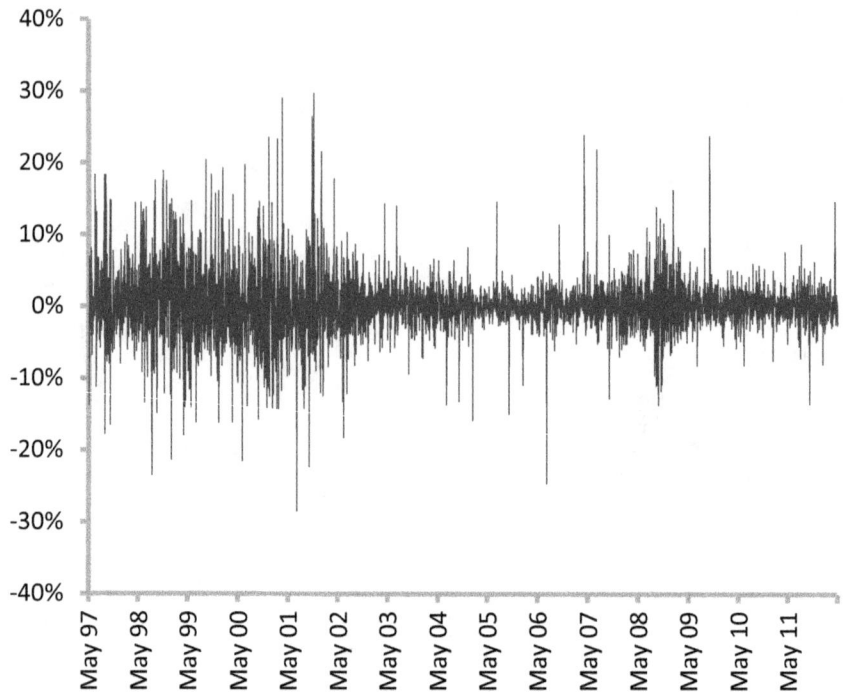

Figure 2.2   Amazon.com daily price movements

The standard deviation of this series is about 3.4 per cent, and a "six sigma" event with a daily move of over 26 per cent would occur only once in a billion days in a normally distributed data set; but there are three such events in this sample of 15 years' trading.

Based on daily close. Source: Yahoo.com

explanation for changes in stock prices is that they reflect new information; J. M. Keynes, an economist and a successful speculator, suggested that the stock market was like a newspaper contest for the most beautiful girl, where the prize goes to the entrant whose choice most closely reflects average opinion.

To win such a contest you do not nominate the girl that you think the most beautiful, but the one who you think the majority of the entrants will think that the majority of entrants will think the most beautiful.

Standard finance theory assumes that changes in a stock or share price represent new information and that at any time the share price is the best possible estimate of the future earnings of the relevant company. The standard theory assumes further that the impact of successive tranches of information is normally distributed. Figure 2.2 offers conclusive evidence that the standard theory cannot account for movements in Amazon.com's share price; and it is hard if not impossible to find a security to which the standard theory does apply.

Once Keynes's insight is accepted and it is recognised that share traders watch each other as well as considering estimates of a security's intrinsic value we would expect that movements in the share price will be distributed chaotically, not normally—and events that would be extreme under the assumption of a normal distribution will occur relatively frequently.

The average change in the Amazon.com share price in the period covered by the charts is 3.20 per cent, but on 26th November 2001 the price closed a full 34.5 per cent above the previous day's close. The stock had suddenly become popular again after a long slide. Earlier in Amazon's history things got almost as spectacular: on 1st September 1998 the stock opened at (an unadjusted) $76.13, rose to $86.62, fell to $65.00 and finally closed at $79.95. Over the day the stock gained slightly but the intraday spread was 33.3 per cent. Keynes wins.

Phase diagrams in physical chemistry and metallurgy are charts where each of the axes represents a physical property. The original phase diagrams were so called because the horizontal axis would represent temperature, the vertical axis pressure, and the chart itself would represent the phase, or state, of some material of interest. At moderate pressures and temperatures, for example, water is liquid (or in the liquid phase). At very low pressures or very high temperatures, water is present as steam: a gas. At low temperatures water is only present as ice: a solid. Rather than a map of the ocean, a phase diagram is a map of the state of some material or system.

Pressure and temperature may be enough to define the state of water, but often there are more than two controlling parameters. Metallurgists will be interested in the temperature of their alloy and the concentration of each of the components, for example.

A rocket scientist will want to know the current location of her rocket, typically its distance above the surface of the earth, its latitude and its longitude; how fast it is travelling, a speed in each of three directions; its angle, another three dimensions; and how it is spinning, rolling and yawing, three more dimensions. She will probably also be interested in how much fuel is left and a number of other measurements as well. A complete set of measurements defines a state of the rocket, or its "position in phase space".

Attractors and trajectories

If our rocket scientist knows all of the relevant parameters for her rocket at a given moment, her computers can use the laws of physics and chemistry to calculate how these parameters will change as time moves on. The rocket's path through three-dimensional space is referred to as its "trajectory", and while its physical position is only part of the total description of its state, language is not stretched too far if we talk about its trajectory in phase or state space.

A couple of points emerge quite clearly. One is that, if another rocket found itself at a point on the same trajectory as ours in phase space the laws of physics and chemistry constrain it to do exactly what ours did. Another is that if the phase space trajectory of our rocket crossed its own path it would then have to repeat the path from that point until it crossed its own path again: its trajectory would become an orbit.

If we look at our rocket at the moment of lift-off we (or its on-board computer) may vary its trajectory by varying the time to engine shutdown and by operating steering rockets. If we examine the complete range through which all the controls can move we can set out a family of trajectories in phase space, and the outermost of these trajectories define the rocket's envelope of possibilities. There will be a highest possible altitude, and a longest possible range, and no matter how the controls are arranged, the rocket won't fly higher or travel further than these values.

The envelope cannot be used to say exactly what a system is going to do, but it will often show clearly what a system is *not* going to do under given conditions. Naval engineers can now produce phase maps which will indicate the operating limits for a boat: they will not know exactly how violently the boat may rock or pitch, but they will know that the boat is not going to founder or capsize in the conditions for which it is designed, which is reassuring.

The path of the stars has attracted human interest as far back as human records go, and since Newton's *Principia* astronomers have been able to both predict and explain the behaviour of many celestial objects by applying Newton's laws. One early and intriguing result was the explanation of why the moon always shows the same side to the earth and why Mercury always has the same side facing the sun. Saturn's rings have intrigued astronomers and lay people since they were first observed, as has the asteroid belt between Mars and Jupiter.

Mathematical astronomers were able to demonstrate that the

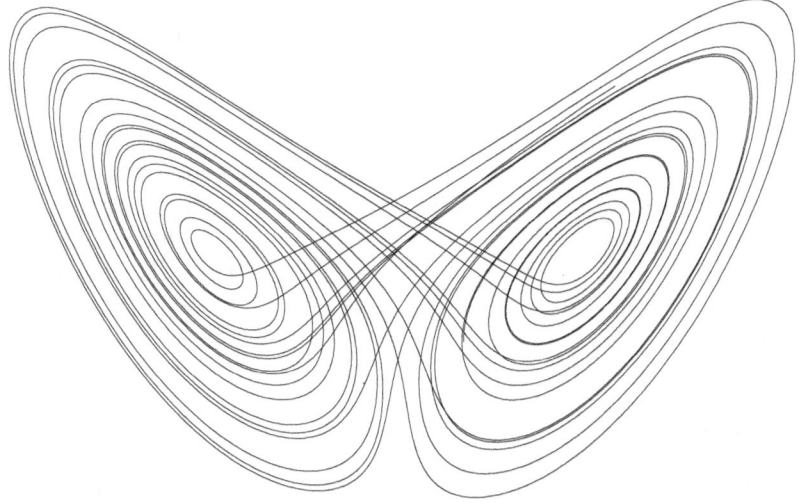

Figure 2.3   Lorenz's butterfly curve

Lorenz had programmed an extremely simple weather model when he came across this curve which never repeated itself or came to a stable point. He thought that it resembled a butterfly.

behaviour of the moon, Mercury, Saturn's rings and the asteroids were all examples of "state attractors": if Mercury or the moon turned faster or slower, or rocks in the asteroid belt or Saturn's rings were nudged out of them, natural forces would slow down or speed up Mercury or the moon, or push the rocks back into their place in the asteroid belt or into Saturn's rings. It didn't matter where they started: the path that they would end up would be the same.

A probably apocryphal story claims that an African language had only three number concepts: one, two, or many. It can be argued that complex systems theory starts from the same premise. A system with only one state variable, such as a weight dangling from a spring, has no interesting properties that were not thoroughly examined in the time of Galileo. If the spring doesn't break and no external stimulus is applied the weight will eventually settle down to an equilibrium position.

Systems with two state variables are more interesting but simple geometric logic shows that they must either come to rest at an equilibrium point, travel in a perpetual cycle, or head off more or less rapidly to infinity. Imagine yourself with a pencil on a sheet of graph paper drawing a continuous line subject to the rule that if your line ever crosses itself it must then repeat its previous path indefinitely. You will find that you must, at some point, stop, representing a two state equilibrium; or settle into a perpetual cycle; or run off the page.

Adding one more state variable brings about a dramatic change: now, your imaginary pencil does not have to touch its previous path when it crosses it: it can go under or over it. We have arrived at a state where a trajectory does not have an equilibrium point, or a limit cycle, yet remains bounded. The "butterfly curve" made famous by Lorenz (Figure 2.3), is an early demonstration of such a trajectory (See Chapter 10 for a mathematical explanation).

Non-linear behaviour

Systems are liable to chaos when their response to some probable or possible form of external stimulation is "non-linear". The decisive test is that in a linear system the end result does not depend on the order in which the stimulation was applied or the time between applications. Every other system is non-linear.

If a bricklayer working on a scaffold calls "look out" and then slops out a cement bucket over the edge he will get one result. The result, from the viewpoint of the foreman standing underneath, may be quite different if the bricklayer empties the bucket first and calls "look out" as the foreman starts trying to get the cement off the back of his neck.

Any situation with a significant decision point is potentially non-linear, as is any where the system develops through a series of discrete events, rather than smoothly passing from one state to another. Systems where decisions and actions effective over widely differing time scales interact are non-linear. Such systems are readily pushed into a chaotic state. Some such systems do not seem to be able to achieve a steady state under any plausible set of conditions.

Imagine the following simplified picture of an investment decision. A multinational corporation is considering locating a major new plant in a small country, because the low exchange rate for that country's currency will ensure that the plant can be operated profitably.

- The multinational announces its plans, which involve a large initial investment followed by a long period of high export earnings for the small country.
- Foreign currency traders will learn of this and place huge

buying orders for the small country's currency, which force a sharp appreciation in the exchange rate.

- The multinational reviews the situation for a few weeks, and then announces that the high exchange rate has destroyed the economics of the project, and they have cancelled it. Within ten minutes the foreign currency dealers unload their holdings of the small country's currency, causing a collapse in the exchange rate.
- The multinational makes another review, and announces that under the uncertain business and financial conditions it will definitely not proceed with the project.
- The small country's government slashes the country's interest rates, in the hope of keeping the exchange rate low and attracting a new project, but instead of selling the currency down further foreign exchange dealers assume that this means a secret agreement has been concluded with the multinational, and their buying orders send the currency up.
- When the currency dealers eventually get bored and allow the value of the currency to fall, another multinational resource company might begin to show interest and a similar, but not identical, series of events will be played out.

This is a non-linear situation, not in the sense of being described by curves on a graph, but by having a sharp point. Under certain circumstances there is no plant being planned: under certain slightly different circumstances there is one plant under consideration. There is no in-between state of half a plant.

Resource and other major projects have a lead-time measured in years, while financial markets respond to news in minutes. A plant such as the one postulated here could wander between viable and unviable twenty times per day as prices change on the stock market, the foreign exchange market and the minerals futures markets. None of these changes actually depend on any physical activity at the mine site or the processing plant at all. Once the ore body has been carefully measured by accurate drilling, and the processing plant built and commissioned, the whole thing becomes of much less interest to the financial markets.

Non linear effects affect the operation of most markets, not just the activities of multinational corporations and governments. Most shoppers regularly confront one form of non-linearity: the stock-out. If the shopper goes to the supermarket first and the butcher second, he may be able to select the last packet of some good that he desires. If the shopper goes to the butcher first, by the time he gets to the supermarket the shelf may be empty. This is non-linear behaviour in the system comprising the shopper and the shop. It is quite likely to have a longer lasting non-linear effect.

Fractals

Schoolboys in nineteenth century novels, and perhaps in reality, referred to classical geometry as "Euclid" because the subject did not stray very far from that ancient philosopher's textbook. Euclid defined geometry in terms of points, lines, surfaces and solids. Each step could be considered as adding a dimension, or measurement: a point has position only, and so has zero dimensions. A line has position and length, and so has one dimension. A surface has position, length and area, for two dimensions, while a solid has three dimensions, which is where Euclid stopped.

Mathematicians have known for some time that there are objects that don't seem to fit into Euclid's scheme. These are sometimes referred to a "pathological" curves or surfaces. They are usually defined by a procedure somewhat more complex than those found in Euclid, but this does not make them any less real. To construct Koch's "snowflake" curve (Figure 2.4) you draw an equilateral triangle, and then stick an equilateral triangle one third as high on each of the sides, and then stick an equilateral triangle as third as high again on each of the sides, and keep it up until you can't see what you are doing. In theory, of course, you keep going until the last triangles are infinitely small.

Koch's snowflake clearly encloses a finite area, but its perimeter is infinitely long: it doesn't really fit any of Euclid's categories, and Hausdorff and Besicovitch suggested that it should be given a fractional number of dimensions; about 1.25 in this case. Following Mandelbrot, non-Euclidean dimensions are usually referred to as "fractal" dimensions and the figures that they describe as "fractal" images. Mandelbrot observed an important feature of fractal images, that of self-similarity: when you examine a small part of the figure it has similar fractal properties, and a similar general appearance, to the larger part. This self-similar property is preserved at all scales.

Nature is much more fractal than Euclidean: consider, for example, the map of Australia's coastline. On a one page map of Australia the coast can be seen to go in and out; on a smaller scale map, perhaps of a particular state, detail that was not visible in the original map now appears, but the jaggedness of the coastline is roughly the same; the

Figure 2.4   Koch's snowflake curve

Start with a triangle; add a new triangle one third the size to each of the three sides of the original triangle; then add a new triangle a third the size of the last one to each side of these triangles; and keep going.

same effect is observed on large scale planning maps; and even if you go to the beach or peer over the cliffs the water's edge is not a straight line or smooth curve either.

Figure 2.5 shows Mandelbrot's eponymous fractal curve: no matter how fine the scale at which this curve may be examined, the part is a microcosm of the whole.

Chaos and economics

The global and national economies are important and complex systems.

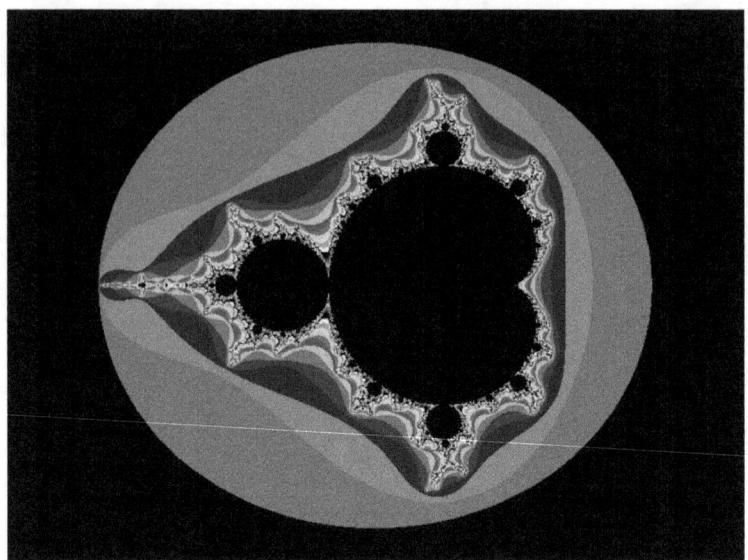

Figure 2.5   The Mandelbrot curve

Source: www.fractint.org

Even the micro-economy comprising a single market or the operation of a minor industry is a complex system. When the mathematics of chaos is applied to economies, markets and businesses some interesting facts emerge. If a businessman has suspected that the Treasury economists were talking about a different world to the one that he lives in for most of the time, he can now call on chaos theory for a mathematical proof of that fact. It was not always like this.

The classical school of economics, initially associated with Adam Smith, David Ricardo and Thomas Malthus, studied change on the assumption that the present state of affairs could be substantially improved. The members of this school thought that markets were usually more efficient than feudal overlords or guild regulations at setting prices and assuring that adequate quantities of produce were available. They did not think or write that markets, or the present state of the world, were perfect, or that unfettered markets should replace civil society. Karl Marx, Alfred Marshall, and John Maynard Keynes[4] were all recognisably members of the Classical school.

The modern or neoclassical school, to which modern orthodox economists belong, started in the second half of last century with Leon Walras[5] and others. These early theorists, men who were familiar with contemporary mathematics and physics, tried to create a rigorous theory of economics that could stand comparison with classical physics as a "hard" science. They adopted the "Principle of Least Action" from applied mathematics and reinterpreted economics in terms of maximising "utility" and optimising the processes that created it. There are a number of subdivisions within the neoclassical school, such as the Neoclassical, the New Classical, the New Keynesian and others. All take it as an article of faith that markets, in principle, produce the best possible outcome for all the participants.

Orthodox economists from the neoclassical school, who are the only ones who get employed by the Treasury, base their theories on a number of dogmatically held assumptions. Some of these are:

- they believe in the *efficient market*, a magical property of markets which ensures that all participants know about every public or private act by all the other participants, "instantaneously". In an efficient market every transaction not only makes each of the transactors better off, but is the best possible transaction that either of them could have possibly achieved
- they believe that the steady state (which they tend to refer to as stability) is the natural state of the economy
- they believe that individuals and households maximise their "utility" and that businesses maximise their profits, and that all households and all businesses are fully aware of all the possible ways to increase their utility or raise their profits and invariably choose the best of these.

When the mathematical implications of these assumptions are fully worked out the idea that the resulting model resembles the real world is seen to be ridiculous[6], but the neoclassical school was saved from imploding by the invention of the doctrine of "rational expectations". The theory of rational expectations takes a plausible idea and from it creates an alternative to the perfect foresight and perfect information implicit in general equilibrium models. People are assumed to "act rationally" by recalling when they made choices with bad outcomes and avoiding these in the future. From this "rational" behaviour optimal, maximising behaviour is assumed to emerge.

A modern orthodox economist rebuts any criticism of the theories he teaches by saying that all other theories of economics and behaviour assume that people are not rational and do not do what is best for themselves. While the assertion is disarmingly simple, it does not stand up to careful examination: the number of choices facing the average consumer, or entrepreneur, is so large, and the time for making decisions so short, that there is simply not enough time to experiment with all possible actions in order to find out which has the best outcome.

There is, actually, plenty of evidence that many people do not act "rationally" in the sense that Lucas and those following him use the term: they may smoke cigarettes, eat too much, drive too fast and generally act in ways that even they themselves do not approve of. When the practical problems of making a "best" choice are set out these, too, seem overwhelming. A medium sized modern supermarket carries 10,000 different lines: this means that there are roughly one googol, or 10^{100} (1 followed by 100 zeros) ways of selecting 35 items for a shopping trolley. If a shopper wanted just 8 items, could evaluate a billion possible selections a second, and started at the time that the Big Bang set off the universe, he would be less than a quarter of the way through the task of choosing the best possible assortment today.

Beyond this practical issue there are at least two critical flaws in the rational expectations hypothesis. The first of these is that choices may interact; that two or more choices must be made together if the agent (economist-speak for person or firm) is to enjoy a "good" outcome, and as long as it is possible for choices to be linked it is not possible for any simple learning algorithm to find the best possible set of choices. The second critical weakness in the concept of rational expectations is the implicit assumption that the correct choice today will be correct tomorrow, that no other agent's choices and no unforeseen event will so alter the circumstances that the behaviour learned yesterday may become inappropriate today.

The very basis of chaos theory is that, beyond the very short term, it is impossible to gather sufficient information about the past to be able to predict the future behaviour of a complex system such as an economy. For this reason persisting with learned behaviour may, and often will, be disastrous. Modern orthodox and neoliberal economists may behave extremely irrationally when objections like these are raised. They may shout and wave their arms a lot, or fling insults, or even fake data and refuse to consider information that might contradict their beliefs. While they may hope to be acting on scientific principles, their behaviour often resembles that of a monk in the most benighted of monasteries in the deepest dark ages rather than that of a rational, modern human being.

When an economist or an econometrician attempts to develop a realistic computer model of an economy or of some part of it, they almost invariably find that the model exhibits oscillatory or chaotic behaviour when it is fed some quite realistic sets of parameters. Some models appear incapable of developing steady state behaviour for *any* realistic set of parameters. Instead of moving smoothly to a new steady state the model may predict quite unexpected behaviour. Increased interest rates may initially stimulate, rather than suppress, demand. A fall in prices may stimulate, rather than discourage, production.

Do the Treasury economists take this as evidence that the world is a complex place in which simple prescriptions may not always work?

Do they what! They change their model.

Any remotely realistic model which allows for the leads and lags[7] as policy changes take effect and consumers and manufacturers adapt to new circumstances will develop oscillatory and chaotic behaviour. Such models might occasionally predict an eventual arrival at a steady state, but they usually don't. Since most economists want to believe that each policy change will have a definite result, they simply eliminate leads and lags from their models. Realistic oscillatory and chaotic behaviour is thereby eliminated from the models, and the economist then predicts a smooth progression towards a new steady state with a straight face.

When the economy heads off in a direction different to the one they predicted, professional economists do not reinstate chaotic behaviour into their model. They rush to discover particular and unique reasons for the deviation, and usually decide that ignorant or collusive behaviour by businesses or trade unions or both was the cause.

Non-linearity in markets

A shopper enters the supermarket and finds that the shelf which should contain his preferred product is empty. The shopper selects an alternative product, and since it is likely to perform satisfactorily, the shopper is more likely to prefer it in the future. Many initially successful consumer marketing campaigns have been destroyed by such non-linear effects: a sound product and a successful promotion lead to a rapid increase in brand preference, followed by an equally rapid decline as the product becomes unobtainable. Even purchasers who preferred the product before the promotion are forced to select an alternative, and the brand share winds up lower than before.

Aggressive consumer product companies have been known to arrange a "stocklift" when a new product from a smaller rival threatens one of their existing lines: agents of the aggressor buy the whole of the launch stock and destroy it, so that any consumers who might have been persuaded to try the new product by its supplier's advertising are unable to do so and are prevented from forming an attachment to it; the small company's heavy investment in advertising is wasted.

Conflicting time scales and intractable non-linearities are continually threatening to force many small and medium scale businesses into an unsteady, or into an all too predictable, state. The raw materials buyer for a factory knows what the demand for his factory's products was yesterday, but must place orders to meet the anticipated demand at some time in the future, possible months or even years hence. The wholesaler knows what was shipped yesterday, but must place factory orders to meet demand at the time of delivery, again, weeks or months in the future.

If the buyer takes too cautious an approach, then buyers down the track will have their orders declined or delayed, and will not return. The loss of customers will force the business into decline, possibly an irreversible one. If the buyer is too exuberant, the carrying costs of supplies will force the business past its cash limits and the bank will put in a receiver. If the buyer gets it perfectly right, the major customer's cheque will arrive before the receiver, and the business will grow and prosper.

A modern economy consists of numerous discrete sectors with many "leaky" and uncertain feedback systems connecting them. A fraction of the wages and raw material payments made by the factory sector return by way of the retail sector. If the manufacturing sector of the economy increases output, wages paid and purchasing expenditure will rise, which may be reflected as higher retail sales, which will encourage the retailers and wholesalers to increase their orders, which means more overtime and higher purchasing...

If, on the other hand, retailers reduce their orders, manufacturing overtime and purchasing is cut back, and manufacturing workers and raw material suppliers reduce their purchasing... But rather than slowly starve to death the retail sector might organise large sales that stimulate demand from the manufacturing workers and raw material suppliers, surplus stock is rapidly cleared and new orders are placed and...

Note that the increased spending power begins to enter the economy at the time the retailers place their new orders, *not* at the time the new supplies become available in the shops. The increased demand may empty the warehouses, and encourage the retailers to place even more new orders.

Before these latest orders are filled, demand may well cease growing because the needs of the purchasing population are substantially satisfied. Retailers may then cancel some of their forward orders, causing manufacturers to cut back on overtime which causes demand to contract.

Whether this type of economy will ultimately produce steady, cyclical or chaotic behaviour depends on many factors.[6] If retailers hold large stocks, and change their order patterns and pricing in small increments after waiting for several trading periods to be sure that a change in the market has really occurred, then the system will probably fall into a steady state or a long period, low amplitude oscillation. These are not the policies pursued by modern retailers, of course.

The drive to Chaos

A well-equipped modern supermarket can change its prices several times a day, if it wants to. For some lines, such stores may carry less than one day's trading stock, relying on suppliers to deliver with a lead time of hours. The well organised modern manufacturing plant operates on just-in-time principles, with no more than a day's supply of components on hand. Like the retailer, the modern manufacturing company is behaving in a way that is likely to provoke chaotic behaviour in the economy as a whole, by minimising its own stock holding costs and inventory exposure.

The question as to how best to describe the behaviour of the real economy cannot be determined conclusively: it may be cyclical with chaotic perturbations or it may be truly chaotic. Parts of the economy can be in one state, while parts of it can be in another.

One of the reasons why chaotic equations can be used to produce such weird and beautiful forms in computer-generated patterns is that the chaotic state itself is remarkably sensitive to external conditions: an almost infinitesimal change in some parameter may cause the system to change from oscillatory to chaotic and back again. Models of business and marketing interactions show similar behaviour, in an even more complex way. The very close proximity of cyclical and chaotic behaviour in such models suggests that most real businesses and markets are moving between one state and the other most of the time.

It is important to note that models in which chaotic behaviour is predicted may be used to predict the *range* and the unpredictable nature of the results to be expected from a particular system. Such models do not necessarily predict the exact values a system will generate at a particular time: often, they state that such an exact prediction is impossible. These results mean that economic and marketing models are of limited long range predictive power. Even when they predict failure through an explosive exit from the market they cannot be used to provide an accurate prediction of how long the system will run before exploding.

Such models are of correspondingly enormous normative and educational power. They can be used to expose and discredit many bland prescriptions by demonstrating that they cannot be relied upon to produce valid results, except in the short term. Many such bland prescriptions start with the presumption that the short term pain that they propose to inflict will be rewarded in the longer term.

Dynamic systems analysis will show that the short term pain is the only certain thing about such prescriptions. The delivery of long term benefits is much more dubious, at least as far the business being advised is concerned. Whether the adviser is likely to share any of the longer term pain is less easy to say. Dynamic models can be used to explore various possible visions of the future, and can be used by planners to prepare a set of contingency responses. They tell us that the world is an exciting and interesting place, where no-one need face the boredom of an infinitely repeated story.

Endnotes

1   Arthur, W. B., Holland, J. H.; LeBaron, B.; Palmer, R. and Tayler P. (1996), "Asset Pricing Under Endogenous Expectations in an Artificial Stock Market", Santa Fe Institute Working Paper 96-12-093, Santa Fé, NM.

2   Lovelock, James E. & Kump, Lee R. (1994) "Failure of climate regulation in a geophysiological model", *Nature* **369**(June), pp. 732–734.

3   Lovelock, James E. (2004), "Nuclear power is the only green solution", *The Independent*, 24 May; Lovelock, James E. (2006), "The Earth is about to catch a morbid fever that may last as long as 100,000 years", *The Independent*, 16 January.

4   Karl Marx (1818–83) was one of the first economists to write about the essential dynamism of the capitalist system. Alfred Marshall (1842–1924) was one of the last great figures of the classical school of economics. His *Principles of Economics* went through many revisions during his life and is still cited today. John Maynard Keynes (1883–1946) founded macro-economics, the study of national economies as overall systems. His *General Theory of Employment, Interest and Money* is now cited infrequently, since it is inconsistent with the neoliberalism that currently dominates academic economics.

5   Donald Walker, in *Walras's Market Models* (Cambridge and New York: Cambridge University Press, 1997) argues persuasively that Walras, personally, was a member of the classical school, although his followers created the General Equilibrium, or Neoclassical, school on the basis of his work.

6   See Paul Ormerod, *The Death of Economics* (London: Faber and Faber, 1994) and Steve Keen, *Debunking Economics: The naked emperor dethroned?* (London: Zed Books, 2011) for extended descriptions of the fundamental flaws of the neoclassical schools of economics. John Quiggin, in *Zombie Economics: How dead ideas still walk among us* (Princeton NJ: Princeton University Press, 2010) offers a comprehensive demolition of general equilibrium theory and various other economic shibboleths.

7   Ezekiel, Mordecai (1938), "The Cobweb Theorem", *Quarterly Journal of Economics* (February), pp. 255–80 may have been one of the first economists to point this out. He supplemented his theoretical description with an analysis of hog belly prices and volumes which demonstrated these effects.

3. Roots and Branches

Random and predictable

WHEN A SYSTEM is behaving in a way that we don't understand we might say that its behaviour is *random*: driven by pure chance. Of course, when we have the time and the opportunity to examine the system in detail, we often discover that there was a cause for this strange behaviour — until we look closer still.

A car may be difficult to start: many attempts are needed before the motor fires. We call this random behaviour, but when we eventually have the car serviced the mechanic discovers a loose connection in the starting circuitry of the electronic fuel control system. He pushes the plug home properly, makes out a bill for $250, and we say that we now understand the problem. Do we? When the connection was loose, it was making contact some of the time, and not making contact the rest of the time. Why? It was a random problem...

Analysing most forms of "random" system response shows this typical pattern of looking simple from a distance and complex close up. We examine the system, and we find some small cause that has pushed it one way or the other. When we examine this small cause, we find again that it could have gone one way or the other, but it was triggered by a still smaller effect.

When we examine the same or a similar system while it is operating in a predictable state, we find that it *no longer matters* what the small and very small causes are doing. While the electrical plug was just resting in its socket, the dog wagging his tail in the back seat could shake the car enough to make or break the connection. When the electrical plug is firmly back in its place, shaking the car short of shaking it to pieces will not cause the connection to act intermittently. The dog can wag his tail or go to sleep: the car will still start on demand.

The word "Random" covers some extremely subtle concepts. The science of statistics is devoted to extracting information from apparently random data. Business planners have become accustomed to treating data as consisting of an underlying value distorted by noise, or random variations. What is more, they expect random events to fall into a particular sort of pattern when a series of them are considered.

Since the very great mathematician Gauss[1] discovered the Normal Distribution Curve in the last years of the eighteenth century, a large body of work has grown up around the concept of "random" and the "normal" distribution. Many strategists and business planners rely on this work to simplify complex problems. Gauss was engaged on a land survey, and *his* problem was to work out when his team had made enough measurements to be confident of throwing out the errors. He didn't want to move his team on until they had taken enough sightings to be confident of their results, but he knew that they had to move regularly if they were ever to get finished.

It is often forgotten that Gauss's Normal Distribution is an approximation to the binomial distribution, making it numerically tractable for large populations. The binomial distribution is accurate if one can accept the idea of perfect coins tossed in a perfectly fair manner, but for large populations involves inconveniently huge numbers; this should be a warning that, taken to extremes, an approximation such as the normal distribution won't provide a perfect fit to reality even all the other objections can be assumed away.

Concepts such as "mean" (or average) and "standard deviation" come from Gauss's work. The Normal Distribution (or "Cocked Hat") curve estimated the probability that a purely random event would perturb a reading a given distance from the true value. Gauss observed that about 70% of the measurements of any survey leg lay within one standard deviation of the average, about 95% within two, and well over 99% within three. The problem he sought to solve was whether he would improve or reduce his accuracy on any particular leg of the survey by discarding apparently deviant readings.

If one reading was four or five standard deviations away from the mean, should it be taken into the average or left out? Gauss comprehensively solved this problem, and statisticians and scientists to this day use his results and some of his methods. Gauss was examining very small discrepancies in very large measurements: his final error on the whole survey was a matter of a few metres in an 80 kilometre survey. Gauss's work on the statistics of measurement was extended during the later nineteenth and early twentieth century to cover many new fields.

Measurement of conscripts being inducted into nineteenth century armies showed that their height appeared to be normally distributed about an average. Rather than do a complete clinical, dietary, family and genetic survey of every recruit, it was assumed that humans are born with a tendency to grow that is normally distributed about a mean.

Overall, military conscription was a good thing for the lower classes in continental Europe. The fact that it was universal forced the

Breeding British soldiers

The First World War confronted the British establishment with the fact that starving the poor and keeping them in noxious slums might be the result of sound economics but was poor military planning, and the seeds of the Welfare State were laid in the conscription queues of 1915 and 1916.

In the event it took a second major war to impress upon the British governing classes the need to ensure that the lower orders received basic nutrition and education. The two needs were combined when compulsory nutritious cooked lunches were made part of the British compulsory education system. British children born or brought up during the Second World War were the healthiest, strongest and tallest since measurements began, and the children who followed were larger and healthier still.

It took until the 1980s for a British government (under Mrs, now Baroness, Margaret Thatcher) to decide that the defence of the Realm could once again be entrusted to professional soldiers. The school meal programme was drastically curtailed and even abandoned in some counties. The health of the very poor began deteriorating for the first time in fifty years.

middle classes to take an interest in the general conditions in which conscripts lived, preventing barracks becoming unhealthy or squalid. The need to have an efficient army (or at least an army that looked good on parade) made the governing classes take an interest in the nutrition, education, and health of the poor.

Of course, lots of European conscripts died when their elders and betters decided to have a war, but the survivors and their families were certainly better off. This point was established when Britain introduced conscription for the first time in 1915 to supply Lord Haig[2] with extra bodies to stack up in front of German machine guns. The poor wretches dragged from the slums of Glasgow, Manchester and London to be sent to a muddy death on the Somme barely reached 80 per cent of the average height of peace time recruits, who had previously been believed to be an even sample of the British population.

People who write about war itself divide into two quite distinct camps. There are those who believe that the result is determined by large factors, such as the industrial strength or population size of the contending countries, or the will of the various leaders. In this view heroism and death are random incidents giving colour to an event whose conclusion was wholly determined by quite different factors.

The late General Chuikov, who commanded the victorious Russian defence of Stalingrad during the Second World War, believed in the large factors. As a committed Marxist, Chuikov wrote that the Russian victory was made certain by the truth of communist doctrine. None of the men who served under Chuikov believed that they could have succeeded under any other general. One lucky shot of the plenty that Chuikov was exposed to might have caused the fall of Stalingrad. Would that have changed the result of the war? Stalin may have believed so. At the 1945 Kremlin banquet celebrating the Allied victory over Germany, Stalin poured Chuikov's glass of vodka for the victory toast personally. Stalin used an extra large glass, but Chuikov still sank it in one swallow.

The First Duke of Wellington stands unchallenged as England's greatest soldier. He took his stand on both sides of the debate at once. In discussion he would at one moment calmly assert that the "finger of Providence" ensured that an army under his command was always certain to beat one under anyone else's. The next moment he would be praising the heroism of several of his men, each of whom held the fate of the battle in his hands for an instant.

Normal distribution

Some of the variation in height between adult males is caused by factors that are so small as to be effectively undetectable except by their effects. When these factors are also unrelated to each other, the result will often approximate a normal distribution. Some of the variation in height of British conscripts in 1915 was caused by such unrelated factors, but much of it was caused by systematic macroscopic factors, and these factors had been concealed and ignored under a rubric of "variability".

Any time when measurements of a population of people or a run of a product reveals variations from a mean characteristic, an observer will find the easy approach is to explain the variation to random factors—a "normal" distribution. Over-indulging this habit can lead to the point where a wide scattering of results is itself regarded as normal.

The concept of intelligence testing and IQ rests on the assumption that there is some measurable property called "intelligence". The average human being has one hundred units of it, and the sort of very intelligent person who designs intelligence tests has over 130 units of it. When the results of a large number of intelligence tests are examined it turns out that about 50 percent of the population score over 100, about 75 percent less than 110, and about 93 percent less than 120.

These are the results to be expected from measuring a normally distributed property.

The only problem with this proof of the validity of the theories of objective intelligence measurement is that IQ tests are constructed to produce a normally distributed result, and rejected when they don't.

True random effects lead to normal distributions, but chaotic processes do not. Pig breeders, for example, are exposed to a mixture of random and chaotic effects. Each piglet in a litter would normally have the same parents, and these would have been carefully selected for their ability to produce large litters with a consistently high birth weight and therefore survival chance. It is not good farming practice to breed out random genetic factors entirely, and so a slight variation in birth weight would be expected. Plotted over a few litters this would probably look very like a normal distribution. The smallest piglets in a large litter may get forced off the teat by its larger siblings, and only get to suck after their siblings have been fully satisfied and the udder is almost dry. After a week or so, these small piglets will have visibly failed to thrive. If the weight of the piglets is plotted at this time, the distribution will no longer be a normal one.

The tiny genetic variation that made one piglet slightly smaller that its siblings will have been compounded by feeding competition. The distribution of piglet weights is chaotic once the link between low weight and reduced feeding for the runts has become an established vicious circle.

The random smoke screen

Workers in the field of industrial quality have had to face and slay the ogre of normal variability. A factory might be accused of delivering 5 per cent defective parts, and explain this away as normal variability. They might even plot their manufacturing errors on a graph to prove that they are normally distributed random errors, and therefore unavoidable. Even when the variation is statistically normal, investigation inevitably reveals that a limited number of macroscopically defective processes are causing most of it. Almost invariably each of these processes prove to be subjected to one or more "system" problems: an honest worker and a functioning machine are producing chaotic variations in their output.

Gauss's normal distribution gradually extended from being a practical way of conserving effort while making very precise measurements to becoming a sociological and economic law. Inferred properties only became "scientific" when it could be shown that they were normally distributed across a population. Even the term *normal* distribution suggested that other sorts of distributions were somehow abnormal, and a little pathological.

At one time marketing theorists used the assumption of normally distributed attributes to come to terms with the fact that new products are adopted at a finite rate. Ordinary human beings can see no problem in the fact that a new product takes some time to get established in the market, but this is a serious problem for economists. According to the standard economic assumptions, the market is "efficient", and everyone who might ever buy a product will know about it soon after it is launched. Why do some people wait, and *then* buy the product?

Probability and the product life cycle

If a product was good to own or to consume, then it would have been good to own or consume on the day that it was launched. Why do so many people deprive themselves of the benefits of owning it as soon as possible? When the history of a successful product introduction and the number of people in each period who bought the product for the first time is plotted on a graph, it looks rather like a normal distribution curve. This coincidence became the basis of a theory that is stated as a fact in many books on marketing.

They describe an assumed human characteristic called "innovativeness", so distributed as to account for the pattern of new product adoption. About 2.5% of the population are supposed to be saturated in the stuff, and so are called "innovators". Another 10% have a reasonable amount of it, and are the opinion leaders. About half the population have *negative* innovativeness. Some people have so much anti-innovativeness that they are called laggards. Only people with high levels of innovativeness would, according to the psycho-marketing theory, buy a new product as soon as it appeared. The opinion leader would not move until they saw what happened to the innovators, the early followers would wait for the opinion leaders, the late followers would follow the early followers and so on...

The experimental basis for the theory of innovativeness rests upon some interviews with some American farmers in the 1920s.

In 1969 Professor Frank Bass showed that the shape of the graph of new adopters over time could be generated without any reference to normal distribution and showed that the pattern of adoption of powered lawn mowers in California could be explained using his

Triumphs of market research — the Edsel

In 1957 Ford launched the Edsel motor car range in the United States. The launch was the culmination of a 10 year program including the most extensive program of consumer research and market planning ever undertaken. The styling alone had taken three years before the personality of the car was deemed to match the personality of the target buyer perfectly. Ford confidently expected to seize 3.5% of the market, or 200,000 cars, in the first year and build from there.

To get the message across $50 million was spent on launch advertising and promotion: a lot of money when the launch could include a television special featuring Bing Crosby and Frank Sinatra for only $400,000 total cost.

Total sales in 1958 were 34,481. The subsequent two years were worse, and Ford cancelled the car and the program, recovering less than $150 million from their $400 million investment.

formula. Many subsequent researchers showed that other product introductions could be explained using a Bass curve.

This discovery took some considerable time to become widely accepted by marketing academics. Twenty years after Bass's paper first appeared the authoritative *Journal of Marketing* endorsed it in an influential review article,[3] and the psychological model is now heard of less.

The theory of chaos has made researchers much more cautious about using the normal distribution as an explanation for any observed phenomena. Chaos theory calls the whole concept of an average into question. The idea of mean and deviation comes from the assumption that there is a "true" value for the property being measured. This true value is being concealed by noise: small, irremovable "random" variations. In the sociological extension of the theory of normality there is a true mean value for a property across a population, but innate stochastic variability causes all individuals to deviate more or less from this mean, average, or "ideal" value.

The mean value of a system in a chaotic state may be changing continuously, and even if the mean is well-defined, the standard deviation grows inexorably with time. How can there be a deviation from a constantly changing point? Even if you know the mean, what good does it do you if the actual state at any given time is effectively arbitrary? The concept of randomness, and in particular the expectation that random behaviour will lead to results normally distributed about a mean, needs careful re-examination in the light of chaos theory and the role of fractal[4] causal trees.

Individual human beings do not act *randomly*. They apply the rules that they have learned to the information available to them. The result enables them to decide on their next action. When a population is offered a choice, they seldom toss a coin (either in reality or in their imagination). The variation among their decisions is the result of series of positive choices based on different people's knowledge and experience.

Both the rules and the knowledge base they operate on changes quite slowly. In most cases, a particular individual, asked to re-examine a recent decision, will re-affirm it. The rules used by an individual may be pragmatic and owe little to either the *New Testament* or Aristotle's *Ethics*. They still seem to be well understood by the individual concerned and are testable and repeatable.

The bank robber, interviewed in gaol, will happily explain why he selected a particular bank, and why he preferred robbing banks to working in them. If asked to judge his past actions, and suggest alternatives, the alternatives selected are frequently simply those that would have reduced the likelihood of his getting caught. He might suggest robbing milk bars or service stations, as being less well guarded. He is much less likely to query the practice of robbery.

The voter, in a keenly contested election, will have definite reasons for directing his or her vote one way or another. Even the dithering swinging voter will have definite reasons for voting for (or against!) each of the contesting parties.

Although the aggregate result of a large number of individual decisions may appear to be statistically random, the individual decisions themselves are not random in any sense. Chaos and random behaviour in a population comes from the fact that slight differences in the rules and the knowledge base between different people will cause a significant difference in their actions. The distinction between randomly acting individuals and a variation of opinion across a population is of vital importance when designing a strategic program for a business.

Mean and equilibrium

The *old* marketing paradigm suggested that the target population had a purchasing characteristic normally distributed about a mean. There was an "ideal" product, which a significant proportion of the population would prefer above all alternatives. At most, a given market in generic products would have a limited number of ideal points. Market research, by concentrating upon a statistically valid sample of individuals representative of some population segment, was believed to be capable of identifying the characteristics of such an ideal product.

The obvious strategic direction suggested to a business by the old paradigm is to make its products resemble one of the ideal points as closely as possible, by physical development if it isn't too expensive, and by advertising if the product is too hard to alter.

Products that did not approach one of the ideal points were believed to attract a statistically deviant subset of the purchasing population only. If this was indeed the case, we would expect to see that there were relatively few different products available, with many firms competing to supply each of them. This is the reverse of the actual situation, where every firm tries to distinguish its products from those of every other firm. The reason for this is that there are no perfectly average people, and so even if one firm occupies an "ideal" point there will be lots of people whose personal ideal is different from that of the hypothetical average person, and who will prefer a different product.

A pathological case arises when there are only two firms competing in a given market: in this case, the best strategy for each of them is to get as close to the average point as possible, since this assures them of half the market, while every other conceptual location must do worse as long as the other competitor occupies the average position. In the more general case it is possible that no firm will find it profitable to supply an "average" product.

An equilibrium point is reached when a number of competing firms find that none of them can improve their performance by manipulating their product attributes or their distribution arrangements, since any customers the variation would gain are more than offset by those that is would lose to its competitors. If they maintain their product attributes and simply reduce the price they will lose more money by reducing the amount that their existing customers pay them than they will gain from new customers. It is quite possible for none of the products available in an equilibrium situation to satisfy the average, or mean, expectations of all the consumers.

In the real world a multi-supplier (but not necessarily a two-supplier — see Box 'Double Trouble') equilibrium loses its stability eventually, because one or more firms will use advances in science, technology or even just market knowledge to introduce a new product

Double trouble

Between 1952 and 1990 Australia's major air services were subject to the "two airlines" policy, with ANA and its successor Ansett Airlines (now defunct), and TAA and its successor Australian Airlines (now merged into Qantas) closely regulated as to fares, frequencies and capacity. Through the whole of this period the two airlines infuriated the public and successive Ministers for Aviation by operating almost identical schedules. Travellers from Perth to Australia's east coast had eight flights a day to choose from, which sounded reasonable until they looked at the timetable: four flights left between 11:00 and 11:06 in the morning, and four more left between 11:00 and 11:06 in the evening.

Each airline's logic was impeccable: if they chose a different time and increased their market share, the other one would move its flights to the new times, while if the initiator's market share fell, it would change back to the old timetable. Whatever the actual flight times happened to be, both airlines would use them.

or a new method of marketing their existing products — an innovation — which enables them to attract a wider range of customers. The introduction of such a new product may be an incremental innovation, in which a new equilibrium may be established with the innovating firm larger than before but some or all of its original competitors still operating; after a period of adjustment a new equilibrium would be seen to be established.

Some innovations are radical, introducing a product so superior to all that preceded it that there is no place left for any competitor who does not match it with an innovation of their own. The economist Joseph Schumpeter limited his definition of innovation to changes so drastic that the innovating firm's competitors had to change themselves or exit the market: "innovations are changes in production functions which cannot be decomposed into infinitesimal steps. Add as many mail-coaches as you like, you will never get a railroad by so doing."

Innovations significant enough to meet Schumpeter's definition disrupt established equilibriums and clear the way for new equilibriums to begin forming. Schumpeter coined the term "creative destruction" to describe this process, and wrote that it was an essential feature of capitalism and the driving force behind economic growth. Schumpeter defies classification as an economist: he corresponded with both Marshal and Walras, making him both classical and neoclassical, but much of his work transcends both schools; it is certainly claimed by both of them. His concept of creative destruction anticipates the idea of order crystallising out of chaos which lies at the centre of modern complexity theory.

Random and indeterminate

Some evidence for the equilibrium paradigm comes from observing the behaviour of the English potato crisp market during the 1960s and 1970s. For some reason lost in history an in depth study of this market was published and has subsequently been used as a source of case study material for many marketing courses and training programmes. It appeared that consumers of potato crisps did not make a careful evaluation of different brands according to complex internal rules before coming to a purchasing decision.

The two most successful ways of marketing potato crisps were:

- mount them on a display rack near the exit from a supermarket, designing the rack so as to make it easy for a small child to collect a bag and drop it into its parent's shopping trolley;
- mount them behind the bar in a pub or club where they could be clearly seen by drinkers buying their next round.

The ideal packet of potato crisps was clearly the most accessible at any particular time. This is evidence to suggest that some consumer convenience products can be successfully marketed on a largely statistical basis. The purchaser in these cases does not believe that there are sufficient significant variations between alternative products, or any significant consequences of making a sub-optimal choice. The instantaneous behaviour of individual purchasers in the potato crisp market appears to be purely a function of their current purchasing opportunity and the strength of their desire to eat potato crisps.

As long as the purchasing opportunity and the desire to eat chips are separate and independent factors, the consumption of crisps will follow normal statistical rules. If these factors become linked then chaotic rules should be applied because normal statistical rules may produce misleading results. To proceed from this demonstration of the basis of potato crisp marketing to the assertion that *all* purchasing is determined solely by purchasing opportunity and immediate need requires an unjustifiable leap of faith.

The alternative suggested by chaos theory is that individual purchasers in every market are making a definite choice based upon the systematic application of some rules, and that the choice is likely to be repeated unchanged in similar circumstances. The rules an individual purchaser uses may, however, be different in different markets, and the circumstances may change in a significant way between the observed first choice and the apparently anomalous later one. Rather than all purchasers being drawn to one of a limited number of ideal points, every purchaser may have a different ideal. On some measurements, most purchasers may converge towards the same opinion. On others, every possible opinion may be represented without any marked statistical preferences.

The marketing paradigm of micro-segmentation is a practical response to observed conditions and trends, rather than developed upon a theoretical basis. It is, however, consistent with chaos theory in a way that the ideal point theory is not. Chaotic considerations suggest that the best strategy for most businesses with complex products is to pursue differentiation and quality. Achieving high quality involves eliminating negative characteristics from the product, and differentiation involves *avoiding* direct competition or comparison with any established products while seeking a spot on the ideal line.

Because consumers in nearly every market are demanding more choice, it is quite possible that the leading brand or product in a market is only the strong first preference of 20 per cent or less of the purchasers. A product that imitates the leader will have to struggle to drag satisfied customers away from it, while a product that aims to satisfy the next largest group of purchasers may find itself the product preferred by up to 16 per cent of the purchasers in the market.

Endnotes

---

[1]   K. F. Gauss (1777-1855) a profound and influential mathematician and scientist.

[2]   Lord Haig was the British Commander-in-Chief during the First World War (1914-18). He represented the nadir of British generalship.

[3]   Mahajan, Vijay; Muller, Eitan and Bass, Frank M. (1990), "New Product Diffusion Models in Marketing: A Review and Directions for Research", *Journal of Marketing* **54**(1), pp. 1–26.

[4]   *Fractal* is a word invented by the mathematician Mandelbrot to describe a particular sort of pattern where a simple rule generates a fantastically complicated result. Fractal patterns can be thought of as frozen chaos.

4. The Strange Levers of Power

He who has the gold

IN EVERY COUNTRY the key to political power is control of taxation and expenditure. In England, the term Prime Minister obscures the actual title of the holder of that office: the First Lord of the Treasury. Even the deputy who assists the Prime Minister in financial matters has an impressive title. In England it is the Chancellor of the Exchequer, with a residence at No 11 Downing Street. In Australia the Treasurer is often the Deputy Prime Minister as well.

The most prestigious civil appointments in England and Australia are the Governor of the Bank of England and the Governor of the Reserve Bank of Australia respectively. In West Germany economic policy was considered so important that the Chairman of the Bundesbank was required to set interest rates and adjusts statutory deposit levels without reference to the government of the day; when Germany joined the Euro zone they insisted that the Governor of the European Central bank be given the same authority.

The finance pages of the newspapers and the business magazines are free with advice to the Government and the monetary authorities. The Treasury employs a horde of well trained economists who are also generous with their advice. Academic economists, whether holding university positions or engaged by think tanks are likewise free with advice on the conduct of economic policy. All these writers and advisers exude confidence in the prescriptions they propose for the conduct of economic policy. Their proposals, they assert, will ensure that the country will move into a long period of prosperity. They all state that other prescriptions will fail to solve the country's economic problems: that other prescriptions will, indeed, make things worse.

Non-economists sometimes note that not all this advice is the same. Often the advice given by two economists is directly contradictory. Even economists engaged by the same think tank or by the same political party are liable to disagreement. The layman with even an ordinary memory will remember that the policies launched with such assurance a year or two ago are having unexpected effects now. Most laymen will assume from these facts that some of the economists must be wrong. Relatively few laymen form the conclusion that *all* the economists might be wrong, yet this is an almost certain consequence of the study of Non Linear Dynamics.

Economics and the economy

The economy is a complex system. In terms of non-linear dynamics, this means that more than two numbers are needed to give a precise description of the economy of a country at any one time. At the same time the economy is an almost fully deterministic system. At the most basic level the economy consists of people and firms ("agents") doing things in an almost perfectly predictable way: at least, it is predictable in the sense that if you observe someone doing something, and ask them why they did it, you will receive a logically consistent answer. If you ask that person whether, in similar circumstances, they would do the same thing again, the answer will generally be, "yes".

A passenger gets out of a taxi, and offers the driver the fare and perhaps a small tip. If the passenger was given extra time to think about it, the tip might be larger or even smaller, but the general principle of paying the cab driver the fare on the meter is quite widely accepted in society. Of course, some people run without paying, but this is a small and relatively constant proportion of all passengers. The economy as a whole is simply the sum of all the microeconomic activities that are taking place.

The fundamental assumptions underlying both the classical and the neoclassical economic models, copied from classical physics, is that our knowledge of the actions of a "representative" agent (in the classical school) or a "maximising agent" (in the neoclassical school) can be averaged and summed to determine the state and the direction of the whole economy of a country. Nineteenth century physicists developed a comprehensive theory of gasses at the core of which was the assumption that every molecule of a particular gas is identical to every other molecule. Advances in physics since have not seriously challenged this assumption — when applied to gasses.

The Austrian School economist von Mises developed a powerful critique of both the classical and neoclassical schools of economists by pointing out that people differ from each other in many significant ways, and the average value of any measurement says nothing about any one individual. Moreover, the larger the population over which the average is taken, the less likely is any single individual to conform to the statistical mean. As will be explained later in this book, von Mises and the Austrians may have gone a little too far in their rejection of statistics and its implications.

Most economists work on the assumption that these small variations cause less than equivalent variations in the grand totals when they are summed and averaged. In one week more than the average number of taxi passengers might evade paying and fewer occasional passengers might use taxis. This might cause actual taxi takings to drop by (say) 0.01 per cent. Economists generally assume that the national figures for economic activity will change by *less* than one percent under such circumstances.

The big picture

Economists are hardly on their own: all of us expect that small changes at the micro level will cancel out on average to leave a clear and steady "big picture". Of course, we are well aware of the possibility of a long chain of causality developing, such as the long story set out in the box below, but we all tend to assume that such a chain of circumstances would be so unusual that it can be ignored for all practical purposes. We should be careful to avoid confusing the impossible with the merely improbable; improbable events become probable if you are prepared to wait long enough for them.

A hallmark of non-linear dynamics is the question of *sensitivity to initial conditions*. This is sometimes called the butterfly effect, from the suggestion that a butterfly beating its wings in Sydney might, in due course, cause a hurricane over Miami. Weather forecasting has been studied more scientifically and with less political passion than economics. What has been proved in the case of the weather is not so much that a butterfly can cause a hurricane. It is that to predict the weather accurately, including hurricanes, for more than a week or so into the future would require the accurate measurement of the weather everywhere on Earth to a sensitivity sufficient to measure the effects of a butterfly beating its wings.

Chaos theory brings traditional ideas about cause and effect into question. Many real systems are, in technical language, *over-determined*. Far from each effect having a single cause, they have many, and given the set of actual causes it may be impossible to tell, in advance, whether any particular one was critical in determining the outcome. If a national or the global economy resembles the weather, then small effects such as the financial fate of a single taxi driver can indeed cause dramatic effects, noticeable at a national and at a global level. A reasonably predictive economic model would have to record every transaction and even every time somebody changed their future purchasing intentions.

When presented with an hypothetical scenario such as that

A long story...

- an unlucky taxi driver is caught by two fare evaders and cannot pay his debts

- he falls behind in his payments to the bank, who decide to seize the taxi

- the driver cannot collect a regular fare, the children of a leading businessman

- the leading businessman takes his own children to school, getting to work late

- the businessman fails to notice that he should authorise a large payment

- an International bank notices that the businessman's company is in default, and assumes that the country is approaching a financial crisis

- the bank sells the country's currency, causing a large drop in the exchange rate

- and so on and so on ...

described in the box 'A long story' it is possible to work out the probability of the final result as long as *all* the paths between the first cause and the effect are noted. Often it can be shown that the chances of something like this happening are far from negligible. Of course, most small incidents do average out and most individual joys and miseries are not reflected in the National Accounts. Sometimes, however, small events may trigger a cascade and alter the course of economic history.

Sand in the gears

Most economists today would angrily refute the charge of being Marxists. When there were Marxists, one of their principal beliefs was that the individual played no role in history: that economics and class determined the outcome of events. "Pure" neoclassical economists form similar conclusions, substituting market forces for class conflict. To neoliberal economists, great men with great resources may influence events, but small people with little roles do not. As a position, this is now no more logically tenable than Marxism. Dynamic systems theory

Economists on chaos

"Multiple equilibria are not necessarily useless, but from the viewpoint of *any* exact science the existence of a uniquely determined equilibrium is, of course, of the utmost importance, even if proof has to be purchased at the price of very restrictive assumptions; without any possibility of proving the existence of [a] uniquely determined equilibrium - or at all events, of a small number of possible equilibria — at however high a level of abstraction, a field of phenomena is really a chaos that is not under analytical control"

Joseph A. Schumpeter

"The threatened wreckage is that of the greater part of economic theory."

John R. Hicks

(both quoted in "Positive Feedbacks in the Economy" by W. Brian Arthur in *Scientific American* 262(2,February), 1990, pages 80-85)

shows that events too small to measure may, and frequently do, cascade up through a system like the economy to cause large and unexpected effects. This sensitivity to initial conditions means that accurate long term prediction is simply not possible.

The large actions of important people can visibly affect the economy, but beyond the very short term, neither the important people nor anyone else can predict what the effect of their actions will be. The same sensitivity to initial conditions that permits the small actions of insignificant people to change the course of history means that important people cannot control the future either.

One of the driving forces behind the development of dynamic systems theory was the need to improve weather forecasts. Lorenz[1] discovered some of the first examples of deterministic chaos during his investigations into this area, and his original strange attractor (Figure 2.3) may have inspired the butterfly suggestion. The field was one in which initial expectations were high. The American physicist and mathematician von Neumann was a powerful advocate of computer development, and his arguments did not go unheard in the American research bureaucracy in the late 1940s and early 1950s. Von Neumann claimed that fast computers would lead to better weather forecasting, which they have. He also claimed that they could lead to weather control, which they have not and will not.

Von Neumann believed that a computer would be able to analyse the weather and determine how a small intervention would topple the weather into a favourable pattern. He knew that a complex dynamic system could be susceptible at particular times and places to small stimuli. What von Neumann did not know was that a complex system could be susceptible to small stimuli at *every* point. Lorenz confirmed that the weather was such a system: ultimately unpredictable and ultimately uncontrollable.

Significant changes in the weather may follow an intervention, but no-one knows, *or can ever know*, whether the intervention had anything to do with it. In some ways it is like a gambler calling for the cards to be shuffled: on the next deal he may draw two pairs and feel that his luck has turned, but he will never know that the unshuffled pack was about to deliver him four aces. A complex system is not necessarily in a chaotic state.

In a steady or oscillating state small variations do cancel out and a disturbance will die away without causing any long term effects. We know, in fact, that economists of the neoclassical school sincerely want the economy to operate in a steady state region so as to save them from the difficulty of coming to terms with the complex mathematics needed to handle non linear dynamic systems.

The most recent research suggests that the successful, or at least the dynamic, parts of a modern market economy operate "on the edge" of chaos. In the stable regions of the space of possible economic states, the laws and theorems of the neoclassical school of economics may well hold, but change is impossible.

In the chaotic region the arguments of the Austrian school would appear to be justified, except that the future would be so unpredictable that entrepreneurs would be unable to implement any scheme for creating an enterprise: the factors that make such a system impossible to govern also make it impossible for businesses to plan. At the boundary between the two regions it is possible for entrepreneurs, and perhaps even enlightened governments, to capture and freeze something from the chaotic region, or to melt part of the frozen region so as to recast it in a different form.

Fortunately for science, if not for the people concerned, the countries of Eastern Europe took part in an experiment which suggests that at least parts of a successful economy are close to chaos all of the time.

Greening Australia

A forestry expert and a green-influenced intellectual were discussing low level scrub clearing fires as a prophylactic measure against major bushfires. The Green person was bitterly opposed to the concept. This opposition did not change when it was pointed out that black Australians had been doing this since time immemorial.

"That's not the same at all."

Black men rubbing sticks together to start fires to clear the undergrowth are ecologically sound. White men doing the same thing with matches are not.

The tests of the theory

Marxism

While von Neumann pondered weather control, a group of Soviet economists and mathematicians saw the computer as the key to perfect economic control. A computer based planning system could, they thought, allocate investment, set prices and determine production levels. They believed that this would produce optimum growth in the Soviet economy and rising living standards for the Soviet population. In fact, the economy of the USSR grew quite rapidly between 1945 and 1961 as the damage from the German invasion during the Second World War was repaired and the armed forces modernised to meet the demands of the Cold War, but there was little perceptible growth from 1961 until 1980 and from 1980 until the dissolution of the USSR in 1990 the economy, and the living standards of the Russian people, were slowly declining.

Why did the Soviet experiment fail?

A lot of explanations are on offer, usually from people with a particular ideological barrow to push. Nearly every such explanation must overcome a counter-example from a successful Western country. Sweden has more social welfare than the former USSR had. Japan has higher income taxes. Singapore had a more onerous censorship system. Taiwan before its reforms was a single party state but it still had a booming economy. The true reason lies in the nature of an economy itself. An attempt at total control of a complex dynamic system involves the deliberate elimination of chaotic and oscillatory behaviour. To the Marxists, and to most people who experienced the rougher edges of the Great Depression, the elimination of the business cycle seemed a good idea.

Why, the Soviet planners asked, build two factories this year to operate at 60% capacity for years? Why not build one slightly larger factory now, and wait until demand is proven before building the next one? Why take the risk that demand might be over-estimated, that one factory might be bankrupted, that the workers might become unemployed? The Soviet planners may not have cared that they were creating a system of guaranteed supply deficits. Since the new factory was going to supply something that the consumers had done without before, consumers could, thought the planners, be persuaded (or commanded) to wait a little longer in the interests of full employment.

The fear of a catastrophic economic depression receded, even in the USSR, as the 1930s slid deeper into history. The very real frustration of perpetual delays and queuing for anything beyond the most boring staples became omnipresent in Russia and in Eastern Europe. The two effects combined to eliminate what appeal Soviet Marxist theory and practice ever had.

What is sometimes forgotten is that Marxism was invented as a way of managing a classical capitalist economy: one in which all but the most basic necessities of life were in limited supply. The planned economy was seen as the most effective way of relieving pressing present misery. To the extent that the USSR was powerful enough to defeat the German invasion during WWII it succeeded; to the extent that practically all Soviet citizens were fed, housed, educated and offered medical care it succeeded; but as a provider of affluence in competition with the economies of Western Europe and North America it was a dismal failure.

The mixed economy

In the period following the end of WWII the citizens of Western Europe and North America recalled the disasters of the Great Depression and, in Britain and its dominions and the USA, recalled the relative affluence enjoyed by the general population during the War, when in spite of strict rationing, conscription and manpower regulation, and in Britain, the attention of the Luftwaffe, the typical citizen and their family were better fed than before the War and the social cohesion made the hardships of war and the war economy bearable. An immediate restoration of the pre-war *status quo* was politically impossible. The policies adopted in the USA, the UK, and the various countries of Western Europe and in Canada and Australia in the years following WWII were far from identical, but they have been subsumed under the rubric of the "welfare state". Key features included:

- Governments committed themselves to maintain full employment by appropriate fiscal (taxation) and monetary (banking) policies
- Natural monopolies such as telecommunications and electricity supply were provided by publically owned enterprises or by closely regulated private ones
- A social "safety net" was maintained including unemployment benefits and free or subsidised medical care, at least for the poor
- Free or heavily subsidised education was provide from primary through to post-secondary qualifications
- The cost of the various social programs was defrayed by steeply progressive income and inheritance taxes

For families that had lived through the Depression, the new policies succeeded beyond their wildest dreams. Even the bourgeoisie tolerated the high marginal tax rates as a protection against the threat of communist or fascist revolution, both of which had seemed all too re-alistic threats during the depression and the succeeding war. The period from 1945 to 1972 saw unparalleled economic growth and diminished inequality: in the UK, Prime Minster Macmillan could tell the voting public that "You've never had it so good"; in the USA President Kennedy could honestly tell Americans that "the rising tide lifts all boats".

The most persistent characteristic of the immediate post WWII period was pragmatism: policies that worked were persisted with; those that didn't were quietly abandoned. In our modern, more ideological time, the policies of the post WWII period are sometimes described as "Keynesianism" but Keynes was deeply suspicious of "isms" and certainly didn't want to found one (see box). The fear of being described as a madman in authority encouraged a pragmatic outlook.

In Australia the conservative parties in the 1949 election campaign denounced H C (Nugget) Coombs, the chairman of the government-owned Commonwealth Bank as a dangerous socialist, bent on destroy-ing the free enterprise system; but immediately the election was won the conservative treasurer-elect, Arthur Fadden, rang Coombs to assure him that his position was secure and that his advice would be required, and

> Practical men, who believe themselves to be quite exempt from any intellectual influences, are usually the slaves of some defunct economist. Madmen in authority, who hear voices in the air, are distilling their frenzy from some academic scribbler of a few years back.
>
> (J M Keynes)

respected, by the new government as it had been by the old.[2]

Pragmatism does not eliminate chaos; but it does limit its destructive potential. A skilled helmsman can steer a ship through stormy seas in spite of the intrinsic chaos of the ocean and the incipient chaos of the steering system. Pragmatic economic management proved very effective in the post WWII period, using both monetary and fiscal tools to ameliorate downturns and temper excessive exuberance in booms.

Two unresolved contradictions within the Western system were to bring the period of the successful mixed economy to an end. One was that policies directed towards full employment meant that there was no "reserve army of the bourgeoisie" (Marx's description of the unemployed) available to limit wage demands; the other was that the payers of high marginal tax rates and heirs to heavily taxed inheritances were able to buy favourable official opinion and to some extent, political support.

The trigger that destroyed the post-war consensus came from the excluded: the countries that had been colonies before WWII gained their formal independence, but colonialism was largely replaced by neo-colonialism. The Middle East had been an Anglo-French project between the world wars, and in the post war period colonial rule was replaced by rule through local elites, with little if any benefit for the mass of the local population. In late 1973 the rulers of the major oil producing countries "slipped the leash" and demanded an economically fair price for their crude oil; at least some of the additional revenue would be spent on alleviating the poverty of their citizens.

The resulting fourfold increase in the price of crude oil led to a doubling of the petrol price and even some fuel shortages in Western countries: workers who had become accustomed to rising real incomes demanded compensation for the increased fuel costs; and employers paid the demanded wage increases and raised their own prices to compensate. Since a substantial fraction of consumers were not in a position to demand increased incomes the rising prices reduced aggregate demand and companies stopped hiring and even laid off some workers. Unemployment rose but inflation did not fall: among the plausible explanations was the argument that the unemployment benefits provided under the welfare state were too generous and the unemployed did not put sufficient pressure on those in work to force a rapid reduction in wage demands.

An alternative explanation for the rise in inflation was the American war against Vietnam: the war was expensive as wars generally are but US governments under Johnson and then Nixon did not raise taxation sufficiently to cover the cost and did not take other measures to reduce domestic demand to compensate for increased military spending. Inflation was an inevitable consequence of such a policy combination.

The twenty eight years of post-war prosperity ended in a decade of "stagflation", with both unemployment and inflation at unprecedented levels.

The return of ideology

In the public and political mind the pragmatic polices that had worked so well from 1945 to 1970 had begun to fail well before the Yom Kippur war in 1973 and the rise in crude oil prices that followed. Inflation is merely a bookkeeping issue for those in a position to demand compensating wage or price increases but it can cause real hardship to those on fixed incomes and those without bargaining power.

The social safety net introduced in the post WWII period in the developed Western nations required overt redistribution: supporting the sick, the old and the unemployed required taxing the wealthy and the employed, and while only a small fraction or the population paid the highest marginal tax rates or saw their inheritances substantially reduced by estate duties that fraction included many opinion leaders and opinion formers.

Some force was put behind the incipient tax revolt by participants in the finance industries who hoped to pocket the revenue flows generated by various state-owned natural monopolies. People and even politicians are brought up to sympathise with the misfortunes of others and to avoid displays of overt greed; and it was necessary to convince them that inflicting pain on the helpless and praising greed in the greedy was necessary; or as English Prime Minister Margaret Thatcher put it, "There Is No Alternative". Mrs Thatcher used the phrase so often that her opponents commonly abbreviated it to TINA.

The set of economic theories that justified cutting support for the desperate and cutting taxes on the affluent become known as Neoliberalism (or in Australia, Economic Rationalism) and the policies based on these theories became known as Thatcherism after their most enthusiastic proponent. Instead of doing what was morally right or pragmatically appropriate, governments consulted neoliberal economists and made decisions that were correct in theory whatever happened in reality.

At first, most people in North America, Britain and Australia found the confidence with which Mrs Thatcher and her emulators, President Reagan in the USA and Paul Keating in Australia, promulgated their new social and economic policies reassuring, and showed this by re-electing them and their like-minded successors. When the International Monetary Fund (the IMF) forced developing and less developed countries to adopt similar policies these caused the collapse of their health and education systems with little corresponding benefit to their economies. Those in the developed countries who criticised the IMF and its "Structural Adjustment" policies for their inhumanity were denounced as "bleeding heart liberals", economic ignoramuses, whose alternative suggestions would have led to even worse outcomes.

The pursuit of policies based on theory rather than reality caused crises in Latin America, Russia and South East Asia; but these could be dismissed by the advocates of neoliberal policies as the necessary correction of the aftermath of poor previous policies.

Only when the blind pursuit of policies based in theory rather than in fact caused the Global Financial Crisis of 2007 and onwards were the theories themselves exposed as faulty. John Quiggin, an Australian economist who had been a persistent critic of neoliberal policies, summed up neoliberalism under the rubric "zombie economics": dead ideas that still drive policy. [3]

The persistence of error

An all too common explanation for the failure of an ideologically inspired policy is to claim that it wasn't applied stringently enough or persisted with for long enough. It is human to refuse to admit to error, particularly when these errors have caused great hardship, including many deaths.

No real economy is in an equilibrium state; but all the various possible equilibria are attractors; it is probable that a real economy has strange as well as point and cyclic attractors. An economy is necessarily in some basin of attraction; but this is not necessarily a good thing. Until the huge economic stimulus caused by WWII the developed countries' economies were stuck in a deep depression with high unemployment and great hardship.

The war, and the adoption of Keynesian economic management

policies after it, jerked the developed countries' economies into a new basin, one in which unemployment and inflation were low and living standards were rising across the board. The attempt by the Johnson and Nixon administrations to fight a major war in Vietnam without raising taxes or cutting domestic expenditure, followed by the "oil shock" of 1973, shifted most western economies into a "stagflationary" basin, with significant inflation and persistent unemployment.

The economies were jerked out of the stagflation basin by the adoption of Thatcherism and the ascendancy of neoliberal theory. The new basin of attraction had high unemployment but low inflation, but also saw unprecedented increases in the level of both household and government guaranteed debt. The Global Financial Crisis, triggered by these unsustainable debt levels, pushed most developed country economies to a new basin but at the time of writing it is not clear what its major characteristics will be.

What has become clear as at the end of 2011 is that the policies that created the global financial crisis are still being pursued. For specific countries such as Greece the result is a return to the Great Depression; Spain is not much better off. Whether the rest of the developed world will sink into the same trough is by no means clear.

What is certain is that persisting with the theories that drove the policies that drove the developed world into the Global Financial Crisis has no logical justification whatever. The outcome is necessarily uncertain, but it is unlikely to be a happy one.

Endnotes

1   Lorenz is a meteorologist whose early work on forecasting led to some valuable insights into dynamic systems. He coined the term "strange attractor" to describe the first phase map of a non-linear system.

2   Coombs, H C (1981), *Trial Balance*, Melbourne: Macmillan.

3   Quiggin, John (2011), *Zombie Economics: How dead ideas still walk among us*, Princeton, Princeton University Press.

5. The Map and the Markets

Hard and soft

ECONOMISTS OF BOTH the classical and neoclassical schools, along with most social scientists, dislike their disciplines being regarded as "soft" by comparison with the "hard" sciences of physics and chemistry. A sound traditional physics experiment has an exact and repeatable result, and economists wish to appear equally precise. The experimental methods used by physicists and chemists generally involve starting with a clean sheet. The history of the components of the next experiment is not expected to influence its result. In their eagerness to be seen as "scientific", economists of the neoclassical school want to start with clean sheet too. They often disregard the history of a society up to the point of their intervention. This leads them to under-estimate the importance of history in determining each individual's actions.

Ironically, the self assertion and brash confidence with which neoliberal economists made their predictions reached a climax just as the global financial crisis struck. This covered the period over which physicists and mathematicians began to study unpredictability. Chaos has been shown to be present in the best defined of physical systems. Denying its presence in something as complex as human society is positively perverse.

Sport imitates life, and in sport, as in life, history is ever-present. When two sporting teams meet, the result of their recent encounters will inevitably be on the minds of the players. The team that won the previous match will start the game with confidence, and if their skill and a little luck leads to their gaining an early advantage they may go on to administer a hiding. If the underdogs, by luck or skill, strike the first blow the top team's confidence may be dented and an upset becomes possible.

The people who make the rules for most team sports are aware that success feeds on success. They do not wish this to continue to the point that the strongest teams establish a permanent dominance over the weaker making every game a ritual slaughter rather than a contest. Most games have rules that deliberately introduce chaos as a way to make unexpected results possible.

Several football codes specify an ellipsoidal ball, for example. Such a ball will bounce chaotically after a long kick or throw, at least sometimes winding up in the arms of the slower or less skilful player. Cricket, soccer and baseball let their games' rules interact with the strange aerodynamics of a spinning ball to introduce chaos into their contests. The aerodynamics of spinning balls fascinate scientists and sports people alike. The forces on a spinning ball are subject to abrupt and almost unpredictable phase transitions, changing abruptly or even reversing with slight changes of speed. Football spectators will remember the balls that swerved, apparently miraculously, past opponents, around the goalkeeper and into the net, but spectators and players alike tend to forget the apparently easy shots that struck the crossbar or slipped past the post on the wrong side.

Cricket and baseball fans recall the balls that dipped and swerved, dismissing top batsmen or striking out leading batters, and turning a balanced game into a rout. The Pakistani fast bowler Wasim Akram taught himself to make the ball swing in an unexpected direction by taking advantage of the minor seam and bowling just above a critical speed. Disgruntled batsmen and partisan English sports writers all but accused Akram of cheating. They reluctantly, and belatedly, apologised after the British Royal Aircraft Establishment showed, using a wind tunnel, exactly how Akram achieved his effect without infringing any of the laws of the game.

Note that the rules and the ball's geometry introduce chaos, not simply a random element. The random bounce or unexpected swerve of the ball causes a significant change in the pattern of play. The break, the sudden turnover, adds excitement to the most predictable game.

An honest player in an unfancied football team flounders in the wake of the opposing star. The star seems to have the ball on a string: the crowd begin applauding his brilliance. Suddenly an awkward bounce drops the ball into the honest plodder's hands (or at his feet). His kick finds a team mate in the open. He cannot miss from that distance, and doesn't. The sense of doom lifts from the underdogs for a moment. The star's aura is briefly dimmed. Sometimes that is all that happens. The superior team regroups and resumes their drive to victory. Sometimes there is another lucky bounce, another goal, and the underdogs begin playing like champions and charge to an upset win.

The difference between random and chaotic statistics is that each random event is separate.

In a random system there is no place for the buzz that the honest plodder feels when he turns the tables on the star. In a random system the star would not be irritated into conceding an unnecessary free kick. In a random system the top team in a league would beat the bottom one more than ninety-nine times in every hundred matches. In a chaotic game the underdogs will get up once in ten or even once in five matches.

Feedback

The systems theorist has a name for the link between one event and a later one. The link is referred to as "feedback", or a "feedback loop". Feedback is a term borrowed from electronics, where the performance of an amplifier may be improved by connecting the front, or output, of the system through an appropriate circuit to the back, or input end. Front and back are terms relating to old fashioned radios, where the speaker gave forth at the front and the aerial plugged in at the back.

The engineer's intention in equipping a hi-fi amplifier with negative feedback is to improve the fidelity of the amplifier as a whole above that achieved by its individual parts. Distortions introduced inside the amplifier are largely cancelled out by reversing them, while the input signal can be faithfully reproduced. Attempts to improve the fidelity of an amplifier by installing too much feedback eventually lead to oscillations at extreme frequencies: instead of high fidelity reproduction the amplifier produces shrieks and hisses.

When electronics engineers want to design an oscillator, as distinct from stopping a hi-fi amplifier whistling, they also use feedback. The circuit they specify will usually include both positive and negative feedback. There will be positive feedback tuned to the desired frequency to make the system oscillate in a predictable way. There will be negative feedback based on overall signal level in order to get a steady volume and stop the signal building to the point where the desired signal is lost in chaotic noise.

In all these cases, the engineer is really putting in a *feed-forward* circuit. The circuit samples what is coming out of the amplifier or oscillator and mixes it with the signal about to go in. There is always a delay from where the output is sampled to where the input is modified. Electricity travels along a wire at a finite speed: about 100 mm per nanosecond, to use units of interest in modern electronics.

Every use of negative feedback, to stabilise an electrical circuit or any other complex system, relies upon the input not changing its nature too rapidly. If a circuit had a feedback wire 100 mm long, and the input carried a sharp pulse lasting exactly a nanosecond, by the time the feedback signal arrived at the input, the incoming signal would have stopped. The feedback circuit, in this case, would go on and inject a negative pulse, causing a spurious echo in the output, which would be

An early oscillator

One tale about the youth of the future engineer George Stephenson states that he was once employed to be the valve operator on an ancient Newcomen "atmospheric" engine. When the beam tipped one way, young George was supposed to pull the rope that opened one valve, and when the beam tipped the other way, he had to let go of the first rope and pull the other one.

After a day of this George looped the strings around the engine so that the beam did the job itself, and lay back in the grass to read. After a few days the owner caught him, saw what he had done, gave him a shilling for his idea and sacked him, since there was no more need for a valve boy.

fed back, causing another spurious echo. In a circuit designed to amplify 1 nanosecond pulses, the designer would be careful to keep any feedback wires short. A wire or other link intended to produce negative feedback can always become a source of *positive* feedback when the input changes too rapidly. This is a frequent source of grief to novice electronics designers and a fruitful source of chaos in the economy as a whole.

A market also operates on feed-forward lines.

Someone purchases a new product because they saw it advertised or were persuaded to try it by a sales person. At some later time the purchaser's acquaintances will learn of the purchase. Later still they will learn of the purchaser's experience with the product. This will form part of their information base when they are presented with a purchasing opportunity. If the first purchaser praised the product that purchaser's acquaintances are more likely to purchase it themselves. This is an example of positive feedback: the more people who have bought a product, the more people who will want to buy it. Sales into a new market where this type of feedback is operating will be seen to grow in a typical compound, or exponential, fashion.

An examination of exactly who is buying the new product is, however, more likely to produce a picture like that modelled in Figure 5.1. The model market in Figure 5.1 is 34 per cent saturated, but this does not mean that anyone in it is 34 per cent a customer. People are users of a particular product or they are not: *nobody* is average. Even when subsets of the market are examined the average can be very misleading. In the regions near an early customer the customer

Figure 5.1   The development of a market

> Each dot represents a customer: because most customers become so after interacting with an established one, the distribution of customers is not uniform. The blank spaces represent potential customers, those who have not yet learned about the advantages of the new product from their friends and colleagues.

population is high, while there are other quite large customer-free zones.

Negative feedback comes from the fact that people either are or are not customers. As more of a particular purchaser's acquaintances try the new product there will be fewer left to make up their mind. The larger the number of customers, the smaller the number of potential customers becomes. In a maturing market there are few people left to be stimulated by observing others, or by advertising, into buying the product for the first time. The success of the positive feedback effects in driving the growth of the market provides the negative feedback that stops the market growing indefinitely. There is no point at which one effect switches on and the other off: both the positive and negative feedback effects are present at all times in the development of the market. The negative feedback effect is much weaker and the positive feedback is much stronger in the early market, because most contact purchasers have will be with non-users.

As the market develops, both forces continue to operate, but the negative feedback becomes stronger, and the positive, weaker. Once the negative feedback has become totally dominant, the market will cease growing, and if no new products are introduced for a long period, will start to resemble the models found in economics textbooks. Competition will start forcing prices down towards costs as customers become more likely to switch suppliers to take advantage of a lower price. "The assumption that conduct is prompt and rational is in all cases a fiction. But it proves to be sufficiently near to reality, if things have time to hammer logic into men."[1]

In some early markets the first purchaser in a relating group of people may be severely dissatisfied with his purchase. It may even cause actual harm to the purchaser or his property. In such cases people acquainted with the unfortunate first purchaser will not buy the product, there will be no source of positive feedback, and the market will fail to develop, at least among that group of people.

Supply and demand

The Law of Supply and Demand lies at the heart of every form of economic theory. As stated by the early classical economist Adam Smith the law merely held that a shortage, leading to high prices, would encourage farmers to produce more and merchants to import more, until the additional supplies forced the market price down again. While the merchants and the farmers were motivated (according to Smith) by the greedy anticipation of selling at high prices, the "invisible hand" of the market would turn their greed into a public benefit by forcing prices down.

As expressed by Smith and his followers in the classical school, there is little in the law of supply and demand to take exception to, but in the hands of Walras and his neoclassical school followers (including the confusingly named New Classical School) the law of supply and demand was asked to assume a greater burden. In modern theory the market price is that unique price at which supply and demand are in perfect balance; high enough to give producers and merchants the exact incentive necessary to provide the exact quantity demanded by consumers, but no more than that.

Mordecai Ezekiel, a late classical economist, objected that the processes of production and transport took time, and so producers and merchants had to rely on their knowledge of past markets in order to make decisions about supplying future ones. Ezekiel pointed out that merchants and producers were apt to over-estimate their own speed of response to signs of a shortage or a glut and under-estimate the speed of other producers' and merchants' responses. Rather than settling to a

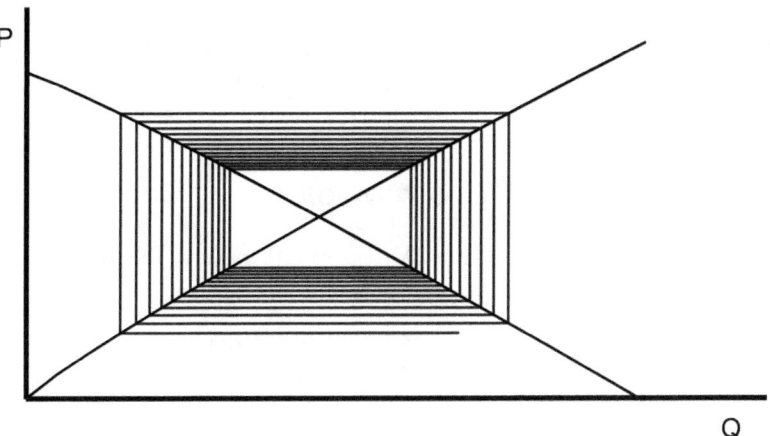

P

Q

Figure 5.2 A cobweb diagram

Because the price does not start off at the point where the supply and demand lines cross, it never gets there.

steady price, the market could proceed in a series of gluts and shortages, so that if the successive prices and supply levels were traced on a supply and demand diagram they would trace out a cobweb.[2]

Figure 5.2 is an example of such a cobweb. In this particular case the forces of supply and demand shrink the degree to which the market price jumps around, but the price never arrives at the equilibrium indicated by the point at which the supply cost and the demand schedule curves cross. Ezekiel showed that prices for hogs in the Chicago market traced something more like a cobweb than a smooth path to the market equilibrium price. The square upon which the cobweb in Figure 5.2 converges is an "attractor"; not a "strange one", but unexpected by anyone expecting the process of determining the price to converge to a single point.

Walras was well aware of the possibility of a cobweb forming, and so he required, as a condition for equilibrium in his system, that it must be impossible for any trading to occur at a "false" price, that is, at any price except the exact point where the supply and demand curves intersect. Walras appeared to recognise that an equilibrium state was an unlikely abstraction, but his neoclassical school followers have largely discarded his caution. They theorise and talk as if the economy is actually at or very close to an equilibrium state. By assuming that every market participant has "rational expectations" of the future levels of supply and state of demand they are able to assume, to their own satisfaction at least, that trading at false prices cannot occur and cobwebs and other non-point attractors do not exist or can and should be ignored.

The orthodox model of a market

To summarise the attitude of Walras's latter day followers to the possibility of oscillatory or chaotic behaviour occurring in a market:

- They hold that the market is "efficient", meaning that prospective purchasers will understand all relevant facts about the products on offer before deciding to buy or not to buy;
- They hold that the only basis upon which a potential purchaser will decide to enter a market or to refrain from entering a market is the question of his or her personal utility or profit: if owning the product will make the purchaser richer or happier than hanging on to the money, the purchaser will buy, and not otherwise.
- As mentioned above, they hold that trading at a false price is impossible; that the "rational expectations" of producers and merchants will tell them exactly how much to supply each market with, including how much each of their competitors intends to supply to each market and the precise response of consumers to the quantities that will ultimately appear.

The principal tool of an orthodox neoclassical economist is general equilibrium theory, with which they analyse an economy "in the long run", effectively eliminating time as a variable of interest. Walras likened the equilibrium state to a calm lake in the mountains, after all the storms had died away. Walras thought that studying the equilibrium state would help gain insights into the behaviour of the economy under stormy conditions, but little of this found its way into his formal work and less is preserved by his followers. J. M. Keynes was bitingly critical of those who only studied the calm long run and ignored the stormy present: "In the long run we are all dead," he wrote.

Storms arise when positive feedback overwhelms the negative dampening forces, and die away as the damping forces gain the ascendancy and the initial energy of the storm dissipates. Feedback occurs in time, and by ignoring time and focussing only on the long run orthodox economists ignore all the factors that created our present economy, all those that affect its growth or decline, and generally, everything that makes life interesting. If anyone wasn't dead when the long run arrived they would soon wish that they were.

A relatively small number of economists have looked at the sources of positive feedback and the nature of economic growth. W. Brian Arthur, the founding Director of the Santa Fé Institute, became famous for his work on positive feedback after an article of his appeared in *Scientific American*[3] and more famous still when he appeared as the hero of Waldrop's book *Complexity*.[4] His fame drew some remarkably spiteful attacks from some other economists, most notably Paul Krugman[5], who had also worked on the economic effects of positive feedback.

The neoclassical school economists praise the market because *if* it works in the manner described in their textbooks purchasers receive the largest possible volume of supplies at the lowest possible price. In general descriptive terms, both the economists' market and the marketeers' market behave much the same way. In the very new market prices are high and unit volumes are low. As the market develops, volumes rise rapidly and prices fall. Eventually growth ceases as the market matures.

When the history of a developing market is examined carefully, it will be seen that every market diverges to some extent from the orthodox economic model. When the way the market chooses between alternative generic products is considered, or how market shares divide up between a number of competing firms, reality and the classical economists' models have little in common. Economists make some particular assumptions about markets. These assumptions let them write out equations which they can then solve. Some of these assumptions are testable by observation, such as the assumption that there are no large firms with the ability to influence prices.

Real markets

In practice, as Chapter 6 makes clear, it would be very unusual for a market to develop *without* producing a marked disparity in the size of the competing suppliers. Some economists' assumptions amount to no more than the assertion that the only possible economy is one which behaves in a predictable way according to soluble equations. For most economists, this means assuming that markets are perfectly competitive with many small firms and no large ones. One of the key assumptions necessary for competition to be perfect is that the price in the mature market is barely sufficient to cover supply costs. Higher prices would mean that suppliers would make profits, and this would rapidly draw in additional suppliers, forcing the price back down to "marginal cost" again. Note that "free entry" is also necessary for competition to be perfect: new firms must not need any licences or special skills or have to spend any money on entering a market that they cannot recover, in full, on exit.

If prices could only cover the cost of materials and wages there would be no way for firms to pay their fixed costs, and so many economists simply assume that firms have no fixed costs. The marginal cost is the cost of producing one more unit of output, and unless the marginal cost is higher than the average cost, even firms with no fixed costs would go broke if they were forced to set their prices to marginal cost. Consider a software company: it may have spent tens or even hundreds of millions of dollars writing its new package, but the cost of making an extra CD or authorising a download from the Internet for a new customer is less than a dollar. If software markets were perfect every software writing company would be broke.

In a modern economy, only raw mineral and agricultural produce markets show any resemblance to perfect competition, but even in these markets the stable or slowly changing prices predicted by general equilibrium theory are most noticeable by their absence. Even with basic raw materials there is a time lag between increases in price and increases in supply, and a less than perfect exchange of forward order information among suppliers.

Operators in financial markets, and in particular, operators in the explicit futures markets, operate almost entirely upon the principle of acting *before* the market has had a chance to become fully informed. Humans are far too slow for modern finance, and the decision-making has been delegated to computers programmed by the best brains money can buy. One of the big problems facing traders, whether automatic or human, is deciding whether another trader's actions are merely routine, responding to a human's order, or strategic, intending to compete a large sale or purchase before the rest of the players in the market realise that the price is about to change.

The trading computers are programmed, on the one hand to divide up large orders so that the large order appears to be a random set of much smaller ones, while at the same time other computer programs are looking for the patterns in trading that reveal that such a division is in progress. The sophistication of these trading algorithms is such that the companies that operate them are prepared to spend large sums on locating the servers close to the major Internet hubs: the ten

Timely information

In the early 1950s, portable radios were something of a novelty in rural Victoria and very few people had seen a tape recorder. When some men entered a pub in a small bush town on a Saturday afternoon with a radio and turned it on, the locals gathered round and heard the race broadcast. The visitors offered to make a little book: the locals were happy to join the fun. It wasn't until the Monday papers arrived with the results that the locals realised that they had still been betting half an hour after each race started.

It wasn't until the police arrived to ask a few questions about strangers with portable radios that the locals learned how they had been tricked.

microseconds that light takes to travel a kilometre along a fibre optic cable might be the difference between winning and losing on a particular trading sequence.

These computerised games would not be profitable in an efficient market, because the other dealers (or their computer programs) would know whether a large buying order was coming or not. It is only by trading on a millisecond by millisecond basis that the trading algorithms can prevent their rivals distinguishing bluff from serious intentions. Even large markets in basic commodities are not always fully informed, or at least, the participants do not show it by their actions.

A new iron ore mine takes about five years to come into production. New Brazilian and Australian mines might be started, each with the planned capacity to supply the whole of the forecast increase in demand. When both mines come on stream, there is an over-supply situation and prices fall below their original level, rising again when some marginal mines are forced to close. Most economists are generally satisfied to describe these fluctuations in prices as meaningless noise, and assume the continuing validity of their underlying model. With some reservations, a marketeer might be inclined to agree—when the subject being discussed is a commodity market.

Industries supplying products with a significant knowledge content, including practically all manufacturing and most service industries, are not and cannot be perfectly competitive.

The flaw in the first principle

The assumption that all purchasers in the market are fully informed

Leaders and followers

At the end of the long Antarctic winter, male emperor penguins pass the egg that they have been incubating to their mates and make the long trip to the edge of the ice shelf in search of fish. Leopard seals lurk near the edge of the shelf in search of emperor penguins. If a leopard seal takes a penguin, the survivors scramble to the shore, but they cannot wait forever for their next expedition or their chicks will starve. The penguins form a jostling crowd at the edge, until one of them dives in.

If the leopard seal has left the neighbourhood, the rest of the penguins dive in after the first one. Otherwise, the process of selecting a new leader continues.

about all the alternative products available, which underlies the theory of the efficient market, is untenable in a market in high knowledge content products. In some such markets, for example, professional consulting services, purchasers enter the market *because* they do not understand what they are about to buy. Few if any employees of any major manufacturing company would claim to know "everything" about their own products and manufacturing processes, and no-one could honestly claim to know everything about every product on the market.

Surveys have shown that most executives with purchasing responsibilities are not even fully informed about the range of prices available, much less about the technical details of the various alternative products. The person-to-person system dominates transmission of knowledge about a market whether in consumer durables or industrial products. Person to person information transmission necessarily involves extensive filtering of information. The first person within a communicating group to make a decision may have studied the subject intensively or may have acted intuitively. The essential information required by the rest of the group is, what was the decision? and, did it work out?

Scaled utility

An absolutely critical assumption made by both the classical and the neoclassical schools of economists is that the differences between individual consumers can be ignored and a large population of individuals can be replaced, for the purposes of economic study, by N

identical "average" or "representative" individuals. When these representative individuals make choices in the market they act to maximise their utility, and if they are able, through an increase in their income or a fall in prices, to buy more "product" they gain more "utility". Economists have recognised for some time that there is no objective measure of utility, but they remain convinced that more of it is better.

Economists of the Austrian school and marketing academics recognise the extreme unreality of the reduction of a diverse population into a multitude of clones of the hypothetical average person, but they tend to draw different conclusions from this insight. Marketers know that different people have widely differing ideals and aspirations. They recognise that the differences between individuals are important, and that products must usually be targeted quite closely to the wishes and expectations of specific market segments if they are to be successful. Some marketeers and successful consumer product firms even suggest that the very idea of a "market" is obsolete. They talk of "mass customisation" replacing mass production and marketing to the "segment of one".

Only when people are purchasing basic personal or industrial commodities will individual differences play a relatively minor role in their choices. The buyer of iron ore for a steel mill will pursue the best combination of grade and price quite single mindedly. He or she may switch suppliers at a moment's notice to obtain a better grade or a lower price. There is nothing ambiguous about the term "better grade" when discussing iron ore: the best grade is that which minimises the cost per tonne processed by the steel mill. Having said it, however, there is nothing obvious in the way a steel mill's buyers go about their job: their costs will be affected by the iron content, the level of various impurities, and the physical properties of the ore among other factors and these will affect their attitude to the various prices that they may be quoted.

The purchaser of a knowledge intensive product like a modern motor car has an even greater scope for individual expression and will act in an even less predictable way. Different buyers will rank issues such as top speed, acceleration, comfort of the driver, comfort of the passengers, ostentation, operating economy and crash protection differently. This list alone allows for 5040 different but equally rational ways for different purchasers to approach the choice of a new car, before even considering issues such as how they plan to use it.

Sometimes a buyer will find out that they cannot afford their preferred car, and they will have to compromise some of their choices. Even in this case they are not conforming to the standard economics

A thoughtful decision

An Australian grazier visited the London Motor Show in 1951, at the height of a wool boom when wool was selling for 'a pound a pound' or about $4.40 per kilogram. This is about $50 in 2011 values, compared to the actual current price of A$9–$12.

The grazier showed some interest in the Rolls Royce stand, but was infuriatingly non-committal as the salesman attempted to get him to place an order. The centrepiece of the stand was a model equipped, among other things, with an electrically driven screen to separate the chauffeur from the back seat passengers. After a repeated demonstration of all the features of the car, the grazier nodded.

"I'll have it", he said, pulling out an enormous wad of currency.

When the grateful salesman had finished taking the order, he diffidently enquired as to which feature had finally convinced his new client.

"It's that screen," said the grazier. "It'll stop the dogs licking the back of my neck when I go out to check up on the rams."

assumptions by selecting the cheapest alternative. They are allowing price to set a limit on their freedom to choose, which is not the same thing at all. Price only becomes the main selection criterion when two or more apparently identical products are the only ones on offer. Even in this case, there are examples where purchasers may not select the cheapest. The lower price may be taken as a signal of lower quality or of dubious provenance.

An interesting possibility arises when a product is good for some people and harmful or at best ineffective for others. If the first person to try it among a communicating group of people suffered harm, then the product is unlikely to be purchased by the others, even those who would gain by using it. If, on the other hand, the first purchaser gained a noticeable benefit, then further sales to members of that group are likely. The more sales that take place to people who gain from the transaction before the first sale to someone who suffers adverse consequences, the more likely the adoption of the product is to spread within and beyond that group.

The dominant form of knowledge transfer is along informal networks, and the role played by the media and by deliberate promotion, after the initial introduction of a new product to the market or idea into the political arena, is relatively slight. The balance between a good and a bad result may not follow statistical common sense much. The female contraceptive pill greatly reduces the risks consequent upon conception and child bearing but involves a slight risk of aggravating a hypertensive condition among susceptible individuals. A very few deaths among pill users had the effect of discouraging its use among a large number of women. The continued good health of women who might have suffered severe complications in childbirth had they *not* taken the pill is not noticed and carries no countervailing influence.

The distinction between information and knowledge is important in modern marketing theory. Information is acquired for the purposes of having conversations and for passing examinations. It is transmitted relatively easily. Knowledge is information that has been accepted as the proper basis for behaviour.

The conversion of information to knowledge frequently requires personal or vicarious experience. The intrinsically slow nature of this process ensures that the development of a market is a relatively complex matter.

Competition between generic technologies

There are two distinct cases of competition to be considered, competition between generic technologies as a means of filling a particular requirement, and competition between suppliers of similar generic

Selling safe sex

The fatal disease AIDS is transmitted by the injection of blood from a carrier of the HIV virus into the bloodstream of another person. In developed countries the dominant forms of transmission comes from drug abusers sharing needles and from sexual intercourse with an infected person.

In the late 1980s the government of Australia launched saturation advertising campaigns aimed at persuading the groups that are at greatest risk to adopt safe practices, notably using sterile needles with drugs and using condoms during penetrative sexual activity.

Studies have shown that these campaigns were extremely effective (as measured by changed behaviour) among the acquaintances of people who have died from AIDS or are suffering from the fully developed disease, and were almost totally ineffective otherwise.

products. The second case is of sufficient importance and complexity to warrant a chapter to itself and is discussed at some length in chapter 6.

Competition between generic technologies has very great economic and political importance, and has largely shaped our modern society. Most economists believe that the outcome of such generic competition is the most economically desirable one, but to do so they must ignore the possibility of positive feedback. Examples of such competition between generic products include the competition between road and rail for freight and passenger transport, the choice between nuclear, fossil fuel and renewable power sources for electricity generation.

When ordinary people assert that the outcome of such a competition between generic products has been socially unfavourable and an alternative outcome would have been better, neoliberal economists accuse them of being sentimental and unscientific. A senior public servant was shown a paper which demonstrated that upgrading a certain rail service would allow a new freeway to have two rather than three lanes in each direction, saving many millions of dollars. "It is not good economics to use public transport to relieve road congestion," he replied.

According to the general equilibrium model competition between generic classes of product leads to a stable balance where each variant supplies the market in the economically optimum proportion. The process is usually described as one of exploiting particular advantages. The equilibrium economist would point to the way in which electricity generating concerns balance the mix of hydro and coal fired power stations on their networks. When a new station is required, the comparative costs of securing coal supplies and of building a new dam are established, and the most economical selected.

Assume for example that the most recent choice favoured a hydro-electric power station. The next time the electricity generating concern examines the question, the cheapest hydro option will be more expensive than the previous one, and the choice may favour coal. On the third occasion, it may be found that the local coal supplies are all committed, and a new coal fired station would require coal to be transported at significant expense: the economic choice favours hydro. This scenario works when each choice is wholly independent or when there are particular benefits from having a mixture of technologies.

When examined in detail, a power system needs a variety of energy sources and power station types in order to provide maximum supply stability and assurance. This can swing the choice towards hydro in a predominantly coal based system, and *vice-versa*. This has prevented a single generic reaching worldwide dominance in power generation. To a first order approximation, in locations such as Tasmania, New Zealand or the American Pacific North West, the choices between generic methods of power generation are independent. In these regions, electricity generating concerns use a mixture of thermal and hydro-electric power.

Such stable combinations of two technologies are rare. It is more common for a "dominant design" to emerge and for its competitors to become locked out. The assertion that the market will *always* select the best alternative says more about the person who makes it than about the actual characteristics of any product.

Forward-linked choices

American pioneers of electricity distribution needed to select a preferred voltage, choose between AC and DC, and for AC systems, select a frequency and a number of phases. Once a given system had been selected for a given area, homes and businesses served by that system had to buy appliances and equipment to a matching specification. Every time a town or district was supplied with electricity for the first time, the choice of distribution standards determined the equipment standards.

Each such choice increased the demand for equipment and appliances made to one standard, and diminished the market share of all the others. The companies and communities making a choice of standards for their new systems naturally took the availability of equipment and appliances into consideration. Fairly early in the development of the American electricity supply industry it became apparent that there were rather more systems operating 4 phase AC 60 cycle, 110 volt distribution than any other single specification. New systems, as distinct from extensions to established systems, tended to treat this specification as a preferred standard.

This in turn influenced the manufacturers of equipment and appliances, who tended to concentrate on the most rapidly growing market segment, the 110 volt, 60 cycle system. Households connected to other systems found that their choice of appliances was relatively restricted and that prices appeared to be higher. Their objections to this situation caused pressure to build up on their electricity suppliers to convert to the common standard, and, on the American continent, 110 volt 60 cycle supplies are now dominant.

There are strong grounds for doubt as to whether this was in fact

The light water reactor

The only form of nuclear power reactor in use in the United States is the Light Water/Enriched Uranium type. Alternate designs, notably the Heavy Water/Natural Uranium (CANDU) and the Gas Cooled Reactor appear to have considerable technical advantages which have justified their use in other countries.

In the United States the first reactor commissioned was a light water design based on the design of a nuclear submarine power plant. The capital cost of completing the design and obtaining operating certificates was such that all subsequent reactors were basically copies of this first one. The market was not prepared to take a chance on an alternative design, and so none of the alternatives have ever been put into base load service in the USA.

the optimum choice. 4 phase generation and distribution was rapidly identified as a mistake, and 3 phase became universal for new systems with conversion equipment installed to maintain service to existing 4 phase customers. In Europe (and Australia) 240/415 volt 50 cycle 3 phase distribution became the norm. This resulted in a 75 per cent saving in copper costs in houses and in the low voltage distribution network in these countries, for no perceptible disadvantage in terms of convenience or safety.[6]

In the late 1980s the authorities in the European Union formed a committee to set standards for digital mobile telephony and on the committee's recommendation the European Commission made the GSM standard mandatory. This meant that mobile telephone users in Europe could use their telephones wherever they went, and because of the high volume production made possible by a single standard, unit manufacturing costs and handset prices fell rapidly. In the USA the market was allowed to decide, and four incompatible standards were adopted in different regions of the country. Users in the USA could not roam freely using a single mobile phone, and the fragmented market and consequent low volumes kept handset prices high.

The market decided on electricity and telephony standards in America while expert committees set the European standards. It cannot be proved that the market did not come to the technically optimum decision, but the evidence is very suggestive.

There are other examples of markets arriving as sub-optimal choices. The VHS and Beta home video recording systems were offered to the market as competing standards. They were launched at about the same time and the equipment and cassettes cost about the same amount of money. Sony had developed the VHS standard and licensed it to Matsushita, but they subsequently decided that they could improve on this design and developed Betamax to replace it. Matsushita had already spent a substantial amount in developing products based on the VHS standard and decided to persevere with it. Many observers agreed with Sony's view that the Beta format was technically superior.

In the event, an inspired piece of salesmanship by Toshihiko Takeshita, the President of Matsushita, secured a major distribution deal for their VHS systems through RCA in the US.[7] This was noted by the distributors of pre-recorded video tapes, a few of whom arranged to service the faster growing VHS market before issuing their titles on Beta. This in turn was noticed by a few prospective VCR purchasers, who began to favour the equipment that seemed to attract the best selection of new titles.

Both these effects were initially very small: Beta versions of new titles usually appeared on the same day as VHS versions, but occasionally appeared a day or two later. Distributors of Beta video cassette recorders advertised and discounted aggressively and initially stopped their unit sales falling more than marginally behind VHS sales. The two stage positive feedback between VHS VCR sales and the number of titles available earlier or only on VHS had nevertheless been established. Sales of VHS systems grew in spite of Sony's efforts in support of Beta, and the VHS standard came to dominate the market.

The division of the market followed chaotic rules, with a small initial variation in share propagating to become a very large one. It did not follow classical statistical rules, with each competitor gaining a stable share according to the comparative advantages of its products.

Endnotes

1   J. A. Schumpeter (1934), *The theory of economic development, An Inquiry Into Profits, Capital, Credit, Interests and the Business Cycle* trans. R. Opie, Cambridge, Ma: Harvard University Press.

2   Ezekiel, Mordecai (1938), "The Cobweb Theorem", *Quarterly Journal of Economics* (February), pp. 255–80.

3   Arthur, W. Brian (1990), "Positive Feedbacks in the Economy", *Scientific American* **262** (February).

4   Waldrop, M. Mitchell (1992), *Complexity: The Emerging Science at the Edge of Order and Chaos*, New York: Simon and Schuster.

5   Krugman, P. (1998), "The legend of Arthur", http://web.mit.edu/krugman/www/legend.html

6   One argument in favour of the 110 volt system is its supposed greater safety. In modern practice, no AC supply above 32 volts is considered intrinsically safe. A victim of electrocution at 110 volts is just as dead as the person killed by 240 volts.

7   Yamashita, Toshihiko (1989), *The Panasonic Way: From a Chief Executive's Desk* (tr. F. Baldwin), New York: Kodansha International.

6. A New Look at Competition

Finding a solid basis

THE STANDARD ECONOMIC model of the competitive market place offers few useful insights into those markets where the products offered include significant knowledge content, since such a market cannot be "efficient" in the economists' sense. Standard marketing theory accepts the consequences of limited product knowledge among consumers, and attempts to predict consumer behaviour according to the rules of statistics. The early marketing models treated each group of consumers as having a propensity to purchase a given product under given circumstances which were normally distributed about a mean value.

From the mathematical, if not the practical, viewpoint the statistical approach has some distinct advantages. Most notably, the consumer's urge to purchase and the marketeer's provision of opportunities to purchase can be treated as independent factors. Chaos research makes the old marketing model deeply suspect when applied to purchases of products of non-trivial significance to the purchaser. It is known that sales of potato crisps in a typical English supermarket can be greatly increased by placing them where children can readily grab them. Factors other than the ease with which a child can add a packet to its mother's supermarket trolley are of considerable importance in the sale of cars, or computers, or even domestic washing machines.

The theory of the ideal point, which will be familiar to anyone who has played the Markstrat[1] game, assumes that a statistical approach can determine a best fit strategy. The theory recommends creating a profile of an average person with the results of market research. The ideal point theory then suggests making the product appeal to this hypothetical average person, assuming that the product development approach does not cost too much or take too long. When, as is usually the case, the resulting product does not completely match the average requirements profile the popular perception should be moulded to the product by advertising.

One major weakness of the ideal point theory is that it incorporates the assumption that a significant number of actual purchasers will react like the synthetic ideal. This is not always true. If half of the real people want a black one and the other half want a white one, then a grey one, while appealing to the average purchaser, might have no customers at all. Another major problem with the ideal point theory is shown up by chaos research. Because people are influenced by their own previous experience and by observing the experiences of others, few consumers actually make a choice that is independent of other choices. When interviewed in isolation, a consumer might specify a product with a particular combination of properties as being ideal. The same consumer, when entering a real market, may purchase a product with an entirely different set of properties.

The history of the Ford Edsel (see the box "Triumphs of marketing research" in Chapter 3) presents an equivocal justification at best for market research led product and market planning. One factor that worked against the Edsel was the high power of its engine. Ford's market research had shown that consumers in its target market segments wanted a car that was more powerful than the rest. At the time the Edsel was launched, road safety had become a public issue in the United States, and leading public figures blamed excessive speed, possibly to divert attention from the impact of alcohol consumption on driving. One result was that Ford was prohibited from advertising the Edsel's major feature, its power.

Some economists' fables about markets

Fable	Fact
The market is efficient, with every participant having complete knowledge about the products, the prices, and other participants' intentions	The majority of purchasers are only weakly informed about prices and alternative sources of supply
There are no dominant suppliers	Even when no supplier to a new market starts off with any useful advantages the market will develop asymmetrically such that some suppliers will come to dominate the market
A market has a single equilibrium point to which the market will always tend following a perturbation	A market has a quasi-infinite number of quasi-stable states. The result of a perturbation may be a change to an arbitrary state.

The other was that Edsel purchasers were associated with a lack of care for the public safety.

Ford's target market for the Edsel was the young, ambitious executive, a group who at the time were particularly eager to conform to the behaviour patterns that would secure their promotion. This group, above all groups, would avoid drawing unfavourable attention to themselves. Although the young executives certainly wanted a car in which they could live out their fantasies of effortlessly passing their colleagues, they wanted their boss's approval even more.

A non-uniform population

The ideal point theory suggests that marketeers should treat their target customers as a near uniform mass, differing only in their preferred shades of grey. The theory of segmentation recognises the gross problems associated with the simple ideal point theory, and suggests that different identifiable groups of purchasers may be grouped around separate ideal points.

To a large extent, this view was forced upon marketeers by the nature of the mathematical and statistical tools available, and in many cases, the limitations of the mass production process. Humans, including many marketing professionals, are very apt to confuse the effect of bowing to the inevitable with a willed choice. Means and standard deviations go back two hundred years, and the multiple ideal point theory relies on the mathematics of the complex plane, something sufficiently well established to be taught to undergraduate engineers. Chaos theory provides a new set of tools that in turn can be used to develop a new way of looking at marketing problems.

Rather than looking at a population as a gently graded mass, with each individual almost indistinguishable from his or her neighbour, the purchasing population can be regarded as sharply differentiated individuals, who buy and use one product or another with enthusiasm. While using the new analytical tools, the old wisdom should not be discarded. Some of the things we know about people using markets are:

- they are very reliant on friends and colleagues in forming their attitudes: people are between ten and one hundred times more likely to act as their friends and colleagues are acting when considering joining a new market than to form an opinion in isolation;
- they are very loyal to their own successful decisions: people

are at least ten times more likely to repeat an important decision taken within the previous year than they are to strike out in a new direction, although when the initial decision led directly to a major disaster the loyalty people exhibit towards it is somewhat strained;

- people in general do not rush to adopt novelties in areas that might seriously affect their lives: harmless, extremely valuable innovations might take two to three years to be accepted by half their potential users, while ten to twenty years is not unusual for less dramatic or more equivocal innovations;

- fear is one of the most powerful emotions, and fear of being thought ridiculous is one of the most powerful forms of fear.

If possible, any new description of a market should include the traditional marketing descriptions as a subset. A fractal view does exactly that. Imagine a tree, with a normal fractal root structure, that has been carefully removed from the ground, washed, and immersed in water. From above the water, only the trunk is visible, as in a primitive and undifferentiated market, there is a single ideal point. If the water is drained a little the trunk will be seen to divide into two or three main roots. This compares with a moderately sophisticated market, in which there may be several ideal points.

Finally, when the water is totally drained, hundreds of roots will be visible. When the tips are examined closely, each root will be seen to be branching into hundreds of root hairs which themselves can be seen to branch when examined under a microscope. This image of the roots of a tree encapsulates the transition from one ideal point to a limited number of ideal points to a market of clearly differentiated individuals.

The stage that a given market has reached will be a function of the urgency of the demand, which in turn will depend upon the nature of any alternatives to the use of a particular market and the relative advantages use of the particular market confers on the user. Under famine conditions, the suppliers to a market in food will not need to differentiate their products, since whatever they offer will be sold. Similarly, when supplying a food market serving the desperately poor there is no call for product differentiation, just minimum pricing.

In a society in the early stages of affluence differentiation occurs at a very macroscopic level. The arrival of the espresso bar in Australia and England during the 1950s presented a dramatic alternative to the traditional "caff" serving large mugs of brown liquid of indeterminate origin. This represented a splitting of a traditional market into two

Sources of purchasing information
(Typical Consumer Products)

Source	Strength	Comment
Public Information	0.01% to 5%	Annual rate at which public information affects a virgin population, assuming a typical advertising and promotional campaign is mounted
Friends and Acquaintances	20% to 50%	Annual rate at which early adopters will influences friends and acquaintances
Personal Experience	0% to 10%	Annual rate at which confidence in the continuing correctness of an earlier decision erodes (in the absence of catastrophes)

well differentiated ideal points. In 1950s Australia the 48-215 Holden and its locally re-engineered successor, the FJ, achieved an incredible 60 per cent plus share of the Australian motor car market. The 48-215 was the first true mass market car to be offered in Australia and established the ideal point in default of any alternatives. When Ford and Chrysler entered the Australian mass motor market at the end of the 1950s they both made only minor variations on the Holden theme.

General Motors Corporation's Australian subsidiary General Motors-Holden made the 48-215 Holden to the design of a compact Chevrolet that never went into US production. Its successor, the FJ, came in two models: a Special (with a go-faster chrome strip) and a Standard (without). Neither of these early Holden cars incorporated features that would be regarded as mandatory today, such as brakes that could actually halt the car from full speed, or a parking brake that would hold the car stationary against a determined push by a five year old child.

In modern Australia the largest selling single model and options combination offered by any motor car supplier holds less than 5 per cent of the market. There are literally thousands of restaurants, and in many cases the worst insult that could be loaded onto the proprietor or chef would be to say that their restaurant was like some other one. Differentiation dominates. Even the extremely successful mass market chain McDonald's has introduced differentiation into its product over the last twenty years: the food and the serving arrangements are accurately standardised in every respect but the individual stores are built to a variety of different designs and some even offer different menu options. This is a significant change from the 1970s, when McDonald's used a standard store design as well.

McDonald's have increased the appeal of their chain by catering for a varying taste in ambience, while at the same time they are strongly differentiating the chain itself from alternative sources of food. McDonald's promotion is intended to get a large proportion of the population to use their store *sometimes*, not to get a share of the population who use their store *exclusively*.

The decision making network

Each person with purchasing responsibilities will draw on information from three different sources when called upon to make a decision.

- a purchaser can draw upon public information: advertising and editorial material, brochures, books, films and television when forming an opinion.
- a purchaser will be aware of the choices made by a limited circle of friends and acquaintances, and aware of any spectacular failures or successes resulting from these choices.
- a purchaser who has already used a market or its direct antecedent will be very aware both of the advantages of the products previously purchased and of any catastrophic side effects they may generate.

People need to economise on their time in an information-rich society, and so a relatively small amount of time will be available for analysing public information concerning the products on offer in any particular market. When a prospective purchaser knows that the purchaser's friends or acquaintances have used the market and bought and used a product, this information will be given considerable weight.

A purchaser who has used the market and made a decision will not want to cover the same ground again immediately, but in a modern society people are very aware of progress, and as time passes people come to believe without prompting that there will be new products, not available at the time the purchaser originally made a decision, and these should be considered. In establishing a new market or launching a new consumer durable product, the crucial parameter from the box "Sources of purchasing information" is the first one. It would be extremely unusual for the most lavish of advertising and promotional campaigns to convince more than 10 per cent of a target market to respond to the provision of public information within a year of a product launch. If - the product is replete with advantages, the market can respond very rapidly once a few people have gone first.

The single most extraordinary marketing phenomenon in Australia over the last forty years was the explosion of the mobile telephony market. The initial promotion by Telecom Australia (now Telstra) focussed on young upwardly mobile professionals, who were expected to use their mobile telephones as a status symbol. The first market segment to adopt it enthusiastically, however, consisted of members of the various home building trades. The Australian housing construction industry is arguably the world leader, and one of the reasons is the unique system of tradesman-subcontractors. While the builder selects the tradespeople for each of the many distinct tasks involved in house building, a lot of the coordination is carried out by the tradespeople themselves. The plasterer will ring the electrician and the plumber to make sure that their pipes and wires are in place before the walls are finished, for example. As soon as one trades person started using a mobile telephone to check on progress, that person had a strong incentive to persuade the members of other trades to get one too.

With different tradespeople urging each other on, the rate of mobile telephone adoption reached 12 per cent per month, seven or more times faster than the rate at which innovations normally considered popular and successful penetrate their market.

When a supplier has the good fortune to employ a good salesman the early customers will include people who trust the salesman and regard him as a friend and colleague. The salesman's recommendation will be given almost the same weight as that of any other trusted acquaintance, and the early sales returns may even exceed the 10 per cent suggested as the limit of the effectiveness of a marketing campaign. The dominance of IBM as a supplier of corporate computing systems from the 1950s until the 1980s was built around the skills of its salesmen (see the box "Trust me") and the company's unstinting support of them.

The new product launch

A new product is launched into a market that has not previously bought or used it. In consequence very little knowledge about the product can be assumed to be present. If the network of decision makers was assumed to be a map, with a light to represent every potential customer, at the launch all the lights would be off. In the next few weeks or months, a number of lights would come on, scattered almost at random over the map, representing early purchasers. These early purchasers will be a mixture of friends of the business, carefully cultivated customers, and a few unsolicited clients who will have responded to the launch publicity and the subsequent advertising and promotional campaigns.

As the launch proceeds, more lights will come on. Some will be isolated ones representing further unsolicited customers, but the majority will be near to an earlier customer as the new product gains acceptance by information diffusion across the network. The sales figures will show a reasonably steady growth, which will be interpreted as the product reaching 20%, 40% 60% of its potential penetration and so on. There is, however, no customer 20% penetrated by the product: each person in the network is either a customer or he is not.

The customer map (of which Figure 5.1 is a model example) would show that in some areas the product has achieved a high penetration, with most people in that part of the network being customers, and in other areas there are few if any customers. Examining such a map can easily lead to the drawing of all sorts of false conclusions. The blank areas might be blamed on poor sales management, or deficiencies in the product that limit its appeal to certain types of customer. The dense areas might draw praise and promotion for the managers involved. Unless there is other supporting evidence, wide discrepancies between adoption rates in different areas should be treated as artefacts of the knowledge transmission process. They are not *prima facie* evidence of any problems with either the product or the sales management. Such maps are typical evidence that a chaotic process has been at work.

Senior management may be tempted to write off the under-performing areas and concentrate its efforts on the areas where early returns have been excellent. This may be the reverse of the correct policy: the high returns from some areas may be a sign that these areas have few uncommitted customers left, while the poorly performed areas are loaded with potential. The first guess may, of course, be the correct one and there may be serious management or product problems, but

Trust me ...

During the days of their undisputed leadership of the computer industry, from 1960 to 1985, IBM took a sales oriented approach to marketing. They were the dominant supplier of computing equipment to large trading corporations. Their salesmen were trained to become trusted acquaintances of the decision makers and recommenders employed by their major customers. In many cases the IBM salesman came to exert considerable influence over these customers and guided them through the series of complex decisions involved in introducing computers to a large organisation.

If an IBM salesman inadvertently guided a major customer into error IBM's very considerable resources were applied unstintingly to correcting the situation: the only thing the customer had to do was to pay the bills.

At least one IBM salesman gave the system an intriguing twist: "Look," he said, "IBM are an honourable and efficient company, but they are *huge*. You need someone like me to ensure that the correct people in IBM are called on to give you the support that you need. If you don't give IBM this next order your status as an IBM Major Customer will be lost and I will be transferred to another account."

IBM won the business.

without other evidence this remains a guess, and not a particularly probable one.

Competing suppliers in a new market

The orthodox economists' model of a market presumes the absence of dominant suppliers, the presence of fully informed purchasers, and hyper-rational suppliers and purchasers who only trade at the unique equilibrium point where supply and demand are in perfect balance. Competing suppliers are assumed to offer identical products manufactured or delivered by identical processes using perfectly interchangeable staff paid identical (and perfectly flexible) wages.

These assumptions do not, in general, in accord with the observed facts. The most important single fact contrary to these orthodox economic hypotheses is that, since suppliers and products are not identical, buyers form preferences for those particular suppliers whose products and service are satisfactory. Since most businesses attempt to supply appropriate products and give good service, buyers are very likely to become the customers of the first supplier that they patronise in a given product market.

When a number of competing suppliers enter a new market, the initial response of the market will be the same as the single supplier case mentioned above: a few customers, essentially at random, will respond to early selling efforts and to the promotional efforts of the various competitors. When the competitors are initially of different sizes, the larger suppliers might be expected to have more friends and more salespeople. This suggests that they will gain early customers in proportion to their size. As these early customers let their friends know whose product they have bought, all the suppliers will experience strong early growth around the locations established in the launch phase.

What none of the supplies have is any real control over the location of their early customers in the knowledge network. The first check to growth will occur when the boundaries of one local influence group clash with those of another. Purchasers who have selected one of the competing products will not, in general, be prepared to consider a

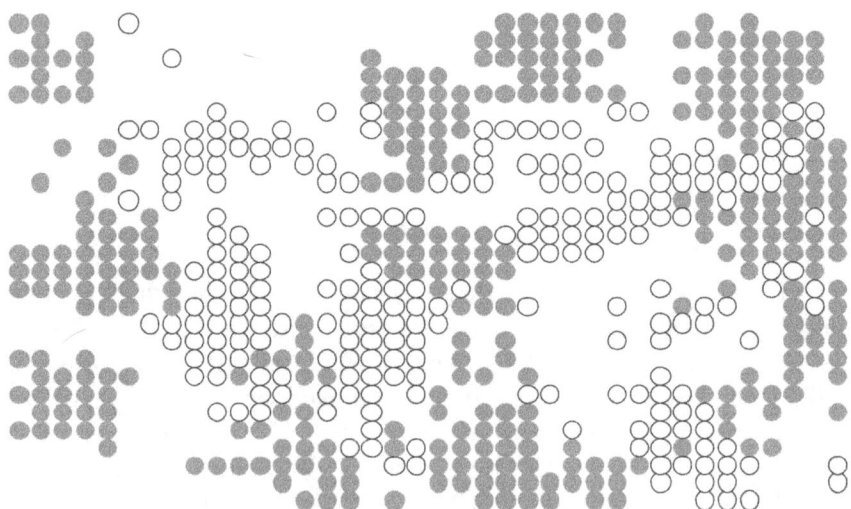

Figure 6.1   A model market with two entrants

This is the same model market as Figure 5.1. The solid markers represent the first entrant, the hollow ones the second. As before, the blank spaces represent potential customers not yet patronising either supplier.

change immediately. Growth of each little communicating group will eventually be brought to a halt when no member is in a position to influence a non-member.

Figure 6.1 models a market with an innovator and a fast follower. When compared to Figure 5.1 the follower, after the four years modelled, has reduced the innovator's share of the potential market from 34 per cent to 29 per cent while the follower gained a share of 22 per cent. Looked at slightly differently, even after four model years only 5 per cent of the potential customers have been diverted from the innovator by the power of competition.

In general, growth after the first clash will depend on the number of customers each supplier has won whom each uncommitted prospective customer knows. Because of the effect of established customers upon the decision making process of prospective ones, the supplier who has the greatest number of customers has a significant advantage over the other suppliers. Only 51 per cent of the potential customers modelled in Figure 6.1 have become actual customers, but most of the remainder are in contact with a customer of one or other of the active firms and subject to those users' influence. Only 6 per cent of the potential users have no committed neighbours and should be accessible to a late entrant.

Piles of sand and piles of money

The mathematicians Per Bak and Kan Chen looked for chaos in a sand pile.[2] If dry sand is slowly added to a heap, the height of the pile rises until a critical angle is reached. At this point, the next grain of sand to fall triggers an avalanche: it is not just the last grain of sand that falls. Bak and Chen made a mathematical prediction of the number and scale of the avalanches, and tested their mathematics with a clever laboratory experiment. They discovered that a simple law described the frequency of avalanches of different sizes: roughly speaking, each time the size of a measuring interval went down by a factor of 10, the number of events rose by a factor of about 3.2.

Their first test of their theory was seismological. The Richter Scale, used to measure the intensity of earthquakes, is logarithmic: an earthquake of size seven involves ten times as much energy as one of size six, and so on both up and down the scale. Bak and Chen examined the statistics of earthquakes as measured by the US Geological Survey and discovered that the were in fact about 3.2 times as many earthquakes with a Richter Scale measurement of at least four and less than five as

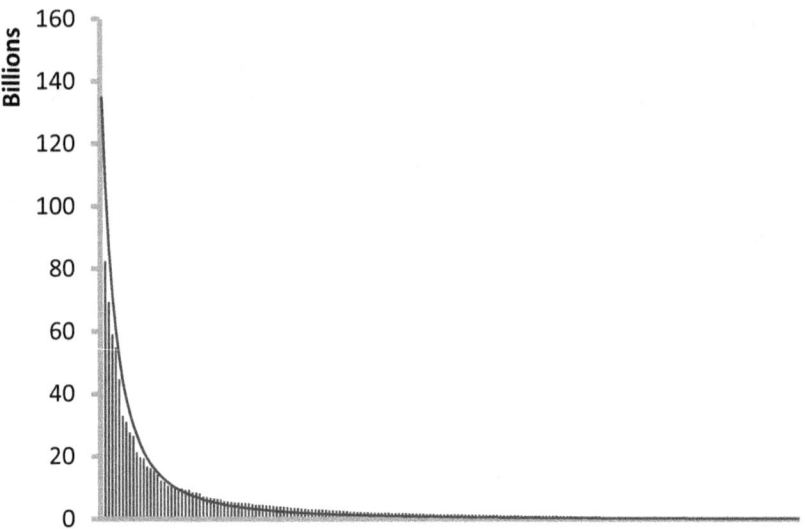

Figure 6.2   Australia's 200 largest companies

The bars represent the stock market capitalisation of Australia's 200 largest companies on 22 May 2012. The line is a "best fit" Bak-Chen distribution with a top-to-bottom ratio of about 1052.

Source: http://www.asx200list.com/ accessed 22 May 2012.

there were earthquakes at least five and less than six, and so on for all intervals for which reliable data was available.

As Figure 6.2 shows, Bak and Chen's "earthquake" distribution appears to explain the size of companies nearly as well as it explains the frequency of earthquakes of different severities. Although the curve does not connect all the bars exactly, the statistical correlation between the two, at $r^2=98$ per cent, is so high that it seems impossible to ascribe the relationship to pure chance. The market value of a company reflects its income earning potential relative to other listed companies, as well as speculation on its future growth and the prospects of it being taken over. Ignoring the latter as creating noise, which should average out over time, a company's value and its income earning potential is largely determined by the size of the markets in which it operates.

While a market is growing the sand pile metaphor is quite striking: potential customers keep joining the market, and from time to time one of them leaves the pile of potential users and becomes the actual customer of one supplier, drawing members of their influence group with them in a logical avalanche. The limits of the avalanche will be set by two factors: one is the arrival of the avalanche at users who are not ready to become actual customers; and the other is when the edge of the avalanche meets the site of a previous one: the potential customers have already become the actual customers of some other supplier.

At the very beginning of the cascade the sand pile process gives some firms more customers than others, with a pronounced bias towards the larger end: although there are more small firms, the large ones, taken together, hold the greater share of the market. Of the firms shown in Figure 6.2, the top nine represent half of the total market value of the 200 firms in the chart. As a market continues to develop, successive avalanches do not necessarily represent new firms: the first person from a group to become a customer of a particular firm may be drawn by that firm's advertising or the convenience of its distribution outlets. Larger firms will, however, be able to afford more advertising and support a more extensive distribution system, and so, given average management skills, an initial size advantage will be preserved as the market approaches maturity.

The mature market

Once a market has matured, which can be well before it stops growing, market shares, in the absence of significant product innovations, are remarkably stable. When some of the customers of one supplier become dissatisfied they will still have a need for the type of product and so will have to choose a new supplier. In making their choice they may respond to advertising or the recommendations of their friends and colleagues. A little thought will confirm that the probability of any one new supplier gaining their business will be the same as that supplier's market share, again in the absence of any significant product innovations and assuming average management competence.

As the market matures, each supplier will find itself in a well defined position on an ordered list. The business, along with the other suppliers servicing the market, will have emerged from a period of strong growth and high margins and may well have been somewhat surprised by the abrupt slowdown in the maturing market. Being a supplier to a rapidly growing market is such a pleasant experience, with the orders and the profits flowing so readily, that it is all too easy to believe that this pleasant situation is not only due to the superior merit of the particular supplier, but that it will go on forever.

The immediate consequence of the onset of maturity is likely to be a short term collapse in prices, as suppliers whose optimism led them to overstock attempt to unload the excess. The businesses that survive this period of market violence need to construct an appropriate strategy. The strategy will have two main thrusts:

- the business must defend its market share from rivals, both large and small, who will seek to grow themselves at the business's expense;

- the business may intend to grow faster than the industry average, either opportunistically or by a sustained strategic thrust.

The sand pile analogy suggests that the position each business holds on the league table at the end of the market growth phase is a matter of good luck at least as much a matter of good management. This will not stop the companies at and near the top of the tree developing a certain smug arrogance or the companies lower down feeling a little despondent. Because market shares are relatively stable, a *definite* effort will be required to change the position a business holds on the ladder.

This effort does not always come from the business going up: every so often a company performs a sort of ritual disembowelment by adopting wholly inappropriate strategies and falls many places. When a business decides that it does not want to wait for its larger rivals to commit suicide, it must be prepared to invest enough resources to destabilise the current market structure: to initiate a round of "creative destruction", to use Schumpeter's term. Of course, a firm that has only modest ambitions cannot be sure that one of its smaller rivals won't try to stir things up, or that the largest firms in its industry will not use their strength to crush their smaller rivals.

Firms cannot, by and large, improve their relative standing *without* an innovation of some sort: a new product, or a new method of distribution, or some production breakthrough that gives it a dramatic cost advantage. The fixed costs of operations bear more heavily on the smaller firms, and their shorter production runs give them less opportunity to reduce their variable costs. This means that any initiative that they take to seize market share from their larger rivals can be overwhelmed by that rival's response, unless their initiative involves an innovation that cannot be imitated immediately. A price cut, or additional advertising, is too easy to imitate to be the basis of an aggressive initiative in a mature market.

Smaller companies do, nevertheless, sometimes improve their position without the support of a radical innovation. The two best chances come from:

- acquiring over-extended ambitious small companies
- awaiting the self destruction of excessively arrogant large ones.

Smaller companies, particularly those with outstanding products, often get bitterly frustrated at the difficulties that they experience in climbing the ladder. They may put themselves in financial difficulties trying to overtake the businesses above them on the ladder, and sometimes may be acquired relatively cheaply. A further chance to pick up valuable share points occurs when some of the larger companies in an industry self-destruct under the pressure of overwhelming vanity. The companies most at risk are those whose relatively high place on the

The wolf on the fold

In 1992 the government of Victoria discovered that the State Bank, at that time the largest bank in Victoria, had incurred losses of several billion dollars in its merchant banking arm. Since the State Bank operated under a government guarantee rather than with a reserve based on shareholder's funds, these losses became debts owed by the government. To minimise the impact on the state's finances, the government sold the State Bank to its longstanding rival, the Commonwealth Bank of Australia.

The managers sent down from Sydney to supervise the takeover acted as if the staff that they had inherited from the State Bank were fools or rogues and its customers suckers who were lucky to have been rescued by a farsighted and caring institution like the Commonwealth Bank. The computer systems operated by the State Bank were scrapped and replaced by inferior systems and the name and logo of the State Bank was removed from all its former premises and all of its stationery.

The former State Bank customers did not respond favourably to these actions by the Commonwealth Bank, and closed their accounts and transferred their business to the Bank of Melbourne at a rate of several tens of thousands per month. By the time the Commonwealth Bank brought its computer systems up to the same standard as those of the former State Bank and started treating its customers politely it had lost more than half of the market share that the takeover of the State Bank had brought it.

ladder owes much more to luck than to any other factor. Rather than being duly grateful for their luck and applying themselves to correcting their product and structural deficiencies, these companies often adopt grandiose strategies for industry domination. Such strategies, when launched on an unsound technical basis, often provide the impetus needed to knock the company out of its relatively secure position high on the ladder.

While going *up* the market share ladder is extremely arduous, and even when carried out successfully tends to happen one step at a time, this is not the case for a fall induced by a strategic misfire. A business that puts its core customer relationships at risk as part of a growth strategy may fail to gain the new customers it seeks and may start losing its established ones as well. There are two ways down: a business can be shouldered aside by an aggressively growing business initially below it on the ladder, and there can be a free fall. The business that is overtaken will generally just change places on the ladder with the over-taker. The business that blows itself into space has no obvious stopping point on the way down. It is quite possible to go from second or third to fifteenth or twentieth without ever occupying any of the intermediate positions.

Regression and risk

A business in a competitive industry will find usually itself on a Bak-Chen line, and for most firms, not at the top of it. When the business supplies other businesses, it will find that the size of its customers also lies on a Bak-Chen line. This can significantly increase the risk of destructive instabilities occurring.

The smoking aeroplane

In 1970, or thereabouts, the Australian public identity Philip Adams called for the provision of non smoking seats on domestic airline services. The initial reaction of the airlines was to refuse, on the grounds that there was "no demand", but they capitulated eventually and designated two or three rows as non-smoking.

In 1988, smoking was banned on *all* Australian domestic airline services, without any protest from the airlines and little sign of objection from any of their passengers.

Much of the marketing literature concentrates on marketing to consumers. The marketing of fast moving consumer goods is particularly well covered. This literature may give the impression that individual customers are of marginal importance in a marketing strategy. It is true that instabilities propagate relatively slowly in large consumer commodity markets. Some future economic historian may see the changes in cigarette consumption in the 20th century as dramatic, when the habit of cigarette smoking among the AB classes dropped from 80 per cent to 20 per cent in a mere three decades. A person living through the change would have noticed that one acquaintance gave up smoking every 6 months or so. Over a similar period, *per capita* beer consumption in Australia fell quite significantly, but again, the change in any one year was not particularly dramatic.

The potential Australian market for beer or for cigarettes consists of about eighteen million people, and no one person in this group can possibly be abstemious or intemperate enough to cause a visible change in a brewer's or a cigarette manufacturer's overall profits and revenues. By contrast, any company supplying capital equipment to other businesses will be faced with a severe skew in the size of its customers.

Most people are familiar with the 80:20 rule. In business and marketing, it is usually stated to mean that 20 per cent of the customers or the product lines or whatever will account for 80 per cent of the revenue. In most globalised industries, six or fewer companies can account for 80 per cent of the worldwide revenue.[2] The single largest company might account for 20 per cent or more of total sales. The largest company on the books of a supplier of capital equipment to that industry might find that its largest customer accounts for 20 per cent of its revenue, and that its five largest customers account for 80 per cent or more. In some industries, such as the Australian motor vehicle manufacturing industry, there are only three firms operating and the importance of each of them to any of their suppliers is obvious. Even in industries where there are many businesses, the sand pile effect means that the top six are still likely to represent 80 per cent of the potential custom.

This fact reinforces the standard management recommendation: if the man from Ford says: "Jump" the correct response is "How high?". Looking after the large customers remains important. It also highlights the relative invulnerability of some businesses to chaotic events, at least over a period measured in years. For an Australian brewing company to lose 50 per cent of its customers in a year would require up to 4 million people to make a decision to change brands, and to make the *same*

Beer and hubris

Bond Brewing tested the patience of Australian beer drinkers after Bond Corporation's Perth-based company took over the Castlemaine-Perkins brewery in Queensland and its XXXX brand in 1985. Bond changed the small print on the can from "Castlemaine-Perkins, Brisbane" to "Bond Brewing, Perth" and nearly 10 per cent of Queensland's fiercely parochial beer drinkers stopped drinking it. Many of them did not return even after the label was changed back to its old reading, and the upstart firm Powers Brewing achieved a substantial foothold in the Queensland market.

decision. For this to happen in the course of normal business activity is so improbable as to make it safe to disregard the possibility. Several public convictions for putting lethal quantities of cyanide into the beer might be needed to scare off half the customers.

By contrast, an Australian company supplying equipment needed in the manufacture of motor cars could lose over half its customers if the chief engineers from two of the three manufacturers made an adverse decision. In fact, any supplier to a single industry is likely to find that 80 per cent of its business comes from no more than ten customers, and in many cases four customers will account for 80 per cent of the business.

Losing half of a business's major customers in a single year would be a pretty improbable event if the three people who made the three unfavourable decisions were making their decision in isolation: a probability of about once per year per 600 suppliers to any one industry.[3] What makes the situation much more dangerous to a supplier in this position is that each of the six buyers representing 80 per cent of the business's customer base by value will know what decisions the others make. The market, in the form of the losing business's successful competitor, will be quite efficient enough to pass on this titbit of information.

The linking of the decision making process will make the catastrophe of losing half of a business's customers in a single year occur with a frequency of about once per 130 suppliers per year.[4] The situation is still more dangerous if a supplier is in a temporary position of product inferiority. Even if it was almost certain that any customer who made a thorough review would stop buying from a particular business, that business still has a better than even chance that none of its six major customers in any single industry will actually carry out such a review in any one year.

If they did carry out such a review in isolation, then the chances of three of them doing so in any one year are about 1 in 60. Because they talk to each other, the actual chances of losing at least three major customers are about 1 in 20 in any one year of severe product vulnerability.

Endnotes

---

1   Markstrat: a computer based game intended to teach certain marketing and managing principles.

2   Uslay, Can; Altintig, Z. Ayca & Winsor, Robert D. (2010) 'An Empirical Examination of the "Rule of Three": Strategy Implications for Top Management, Marketers, and Investors', *Journal of Marketing* 74(2, March)

3   Assuming that large purchasers review the status of about a tenth of their regular suppliers every year, and that a current supplier has a fifty/fifty chance of retaining the business as a result of such a review, this is the probability of a net adverse change of three or more customers from a key group of six.

4   The same as in endnote 3 plus the probability of additional reviews taking place among the six key customers because of the random decision of one or two of them.

7. The Hills and the Valleys

The origins of order

THIS SECTION TAKES its title from a profound book by Stuart Kauffman, an American mathematician and biologist.[1] Kauffman set himself a number of difficult tasks, all centred on the emergence of order from chaos in the most literal sense. Two of the questions he asked are: How could even the most primitive single celled creature emerge from the primeval ooze? and, How did that primitive single-celled organism come to be the ultimate ancestor of the rich diversity of life that we know today?

The answers go well beyond academic curiosity. Kauffman suggested an answer to the first question by setting out the concept of an autocatalytic set, a primitive bootstrapping mechanism. Suppose that, in a primordial alphabet soup, if AB is present then C and D are more likely to combine; and if CD is present then E and F are more likely to combine until the circle eventually closes such that if YZ is present then A and B are more likely to combine. A common argument against the spontaneous origin of life is that the random assembly of simple molecules into complex biological ones is so improbable as to be fairly considered impossible. Kauffman showed that even very inefficient autocatalytic sets work quite fast enough to match the speed of the origin of life to the geological record.

When applied to the normal operations of a business in a developed country the autocatalytic set is little more than an interesting fable. There are two cases where it becomes much more important. The first is when a business originating in a developed country is setting up operations in a less developed country. Managers who are used to grabbing the Yellow Pages™ or diving into the Internet whenever they need a component or a skill may freak out when trying to operate in a country that is largely without telephones. Managers experienced in such tasks become hyper-sensitive to the word "assume". Assumptions can be deeply misleading even when a business from one developed country is setting up operations in another one. They are usually a signpost to the road to disaster when a business from a developed country is commencing operations for the first time in a less developed country.

The general failure of those who advised the Russian leadership to take the need for bootstrapping into account in the conversion of the former Soviet command economy into a market one had tragic consequences. No single skill may be as important to a market economy as that of the humble book keeper. Every business in a market economy needs at least one person to keep track of the receipts, watch the cash balances, and pay the bills, even if only on a part time basis. Elementary accounting is routinely taught in schools in the developed western countries and do-it-yourself kits are readily available from stationers. In 1990 the former Soviet Union had perhaps 3000 people with a rudimentary understanding of book keeping, and yet the economic reformers rushed to privatise the command economy and fragment it into literally millions of enterprises. Fervent advocates of the market economy like Mrs (now Baroness) Thatcher thought that the process of transforming Russia into a market economy would take twenty five careful years. The gung-ho young Russian economists and their western advisers decided to do it in six months: they assumed that market forces would conjure up the skills needed to make a market economy work. Nine years later, faced with a collapsing economy and a growing popular revolt, the young Russian economists were still complaining that the reforms had not been drastic enough: market forces would have conjured up the 20 million missing book keepers if only they had been allowed to work...

Rough terrain

Kauffman's most interesting innovation, from a general business perspective, is the concept of the complex landscape and the consequences that flow from it. Businesses in a capitalist economy cannot stand still: they must move forwards or drift backwards. Progress depends on innovation, in Schumpeter's term a "new combination" of pre-existing materials, components and concepts. The difficulty with developing such a new combination is that elements of the new combination interact with each other. These interactions can be constructive or the reverse, or even ambiguous in that some quantity will make things better but more or less will make things worse.

Consider, as a practical matter, a small manufacturer considering the purchase of a sophisticated numerically controlled machine. The machine can't, of course, be simply plugged in and switched on: someone will have to learn to program it; upstream processes may have to be changed in order to meet the new machine's input specifications; and the machine's output will need different handling to that of the old manual process, meaning staff must be retrained. Automatic machinery is often very productive, so a sales person may have to be recruited to find customers for the extra output. The business will now be more capital intensive, with higher fixed and lower variable costs than before, so upturns and downturns in the wider economy will have a much stronger impact on the firm's cash flow that before.

All these considerations make the decision making process a complicated and uncertain one. There is no simple, infallible rule that a business's managers can use when choosing between alternative ways to develop their business. Once "things have had time to hammer logic into men" people may start believing that they have, indeed, found an infallible rule, one that makes their decision making routine. The longer that this rule appears to work the more convinced the firm's managers will become that they have grasped the secret of success. This means that they may lose the ability to change when circumstances change, and newer, more agile and less hidebound rivals may overtake them. The ancient Greeks had a term for men who believed that they had attained perfection: hubris. Hubris, however, had an inseparable companion: Nemesis.

Kauffman built on work by physicists to develop and study a general model of complexity, one that incorporated "frustration". A system is "frustrated" if moving one component to its ideal location or state forces some other component into a less ideal location or state. The model describes a complex "landscape" within which change takes place. Progress consists of moving to a higher point on the landscape. Unlike our familiar three dimensional landscapes, Kauffman's landscape has many dimensions, one for every possible set of choices; but the basic concept of climbing up or sliding back remains unchanged.

Mountain climbing

The theory of complex landscapes makes the creation of a new business and even the development of many existing ones something like trying to climb a mountain in thick fog. The simplest rule is to look as far as the fog will let you, and then move towards the highest point. From that point you will be able to see parts of the terrain that were previously hidden, and so you can work out your next step from there. This climbing process is analogous to looking at a business and finding some single thing that could be improved without forcing changes to anything else.

In recent times Japanese manufacturing industry, under the slogan *kaizen* or the "The way of improvement" showed that these single small actions could add up to a major change: "the journey of a thousand miles starts with a single step." During the 1970s the staff and workers at Toyota's Japanese factories honed the production process until their plants were twice as productive as American or Australian plants, even though the equipment in each plant was similar and often identical to the equivalent unit in the others. In parallel with this improvement in productivity the Japanese, again led by Toyota, reorganised the quality control systems in their manufacturing plants so as to minimise manufacturing defects and the consequent need for rework.

This time a series of small steps brought Japanese manufacturing quality up dramatically. The world wide automobile industry had been used to introducing a major defect to 10 per cent or so of cars during production, to be detected at the end of the production line and corrected in a rework area, and six or so minor defects in every car shipped, to be corrected under warranty if the owner complained loudly enough. Toyota abolished the rework area by reducing the number of major defects to zero, and slashed warranty costs by cutting the number of minor defects to less than one per car.

Initially many western observers thought that there was something special in the Japanese character that enables them to work so accurately and efficiently, but when Toyota and Matsushita took over plants, complete with work force, that had failed under American management, from General Motors and Motorola respectively, the plants' productivity and quality rapidly rose to Japanese levels.

By the early 1980s Toyota found that there was very little more to be gained from the one step at a time approach. Getting the number of defects per car down from six to less than one was a startling improvement, but there was no way to reduce the number of defects below zero. Toyota's production lines flowed smoothly with no delays and no rework, and again there were no further gains to be made from identifying and removing problems. Using the mountain climbing analogy, Toyota had got to the top and everywhere they looked the path went down.

This is not to say that further improvement was impossible; just that the next improvement would need more than one change. Toyota had to leave the mountain top and descend into the foggy valleys in order to find a route that led up a higher mountain. *Kaizen* could still work its magic, but it needed a new mountain to climb.

Toyota redefined the way its factories worked. They introduced *kanban*, or just in time production, and "lean production", making some of its suppliers responsible for substantial sub-assemblies and reducing the status of their remaining suppliers to subcontractors. Previously Toyota had bought its manufacturing equipment and even its plant designs from catalogues offered by other firms: now Toyota specified the equipment it needed and designed new plants to take advantage of it. The American and European manufacturers who had painfully copied *kaizen* and quality circles to get their defect rate down and their productivity up to Toyota's level suddenly saw the goalposts move: as they reached thirty man hours per car Toyota started achieving fifteen.

Kauffman, whose scientific roots are in biology and whose primary interest was in evolution, described the step by step or *kaizen* process as an "adaptive walk" and the major innovations such as *kanban* and lean production as "evolutionary leaps."

An adaptive walk in nature resembles, on a much slower timescale, *kaizen* in manufacturing. The combination of sexual reproduction and background mutations means that in every generation there are some individuals that have a characteristic previously unknown to that species. They are a new combination of proteins, enzymes, hormones and the other components of a living creature. This will make them more or less "fit" than the average member of their species, and in the rare event that they are genuinely more fit they will have more breeding opportunities. On time scales of a few thousand years in nature, but only a few years in manufacturing, a very small advantage can lead to the descendants of the mutated individual completely displacing the descendants of its contemporaries. The species, or the firm, has taken another step up its evolutionary mountain.

Kauffman deduced two critical statistics about mountain climbing: one reproduced the "experience law" of Henderson and Wright; and the other established that there was an "evolutionary catastrophe" at the top of every mountain. The experience law states that progress slows down as the top of the mountain gets closer, such that getting close to the top is a relatively quick process, but covering the last few steps can take forever. The evolutionary catastrophe explains that, even if the top of the mountain is attained, a species that retains the ability to adapt to future changes cannot stay there.

The changing landscape

Enthusiasts who set out to climb mountains are generally and reasonably confident that the mountain will still be there when they get to it. Businesses, however, change their environment by their very success in exploiting it. The business landscape is a little like a slow motion bouncing castle: the landscape deforms as businesses move across it. In nature the resulting effect is often represented by a co-evolutionary model. Rabbits breed cunning foxes; foxes breed fast rabbits. Slow rabbits get eaten and produce no offspring, while dumb foxes starve and also go unrepresented in the next generation.

Much of the dynamism of a capitalist market economy arises from the interaction between individual firms and industries and the overall landscape. Schumpeter gave the name "creative destruction" to the process of industrial innovation. One firm leads the formation of a new industry, but the mountain that it is climbing is defined by the needs of consumers for its products. As the new industry develops two other effects come into play: one is the growth of separate, but related opportunities; and the other is the erosion of the customer base that supported various older industries.

The invention of the transistor by Shockley and his associates at Bell Laboratories in 1947 started an avalanche that led to the creation of vast new industries and the elimination of several apparently well established ones. The vacuum tube (valve) industry was an obvious casualty, but so were the slide rule and mechanical calculator industries. Electromechanical telephone exchanges and their stepping relays stepped into history; the crossbar exchange rose and fell, and the all-electronic programmed exchanges came to dominate the telecommunications industry. Even these will vanish as the Internet becomes ubiquitous and messages, including pictures as well as sound, are routed over adaptive networks rather than travelling along well-defined circuits.

Shockley probably did not realise that one of the consequences of his invention would be that at the beginning of the following century young men would drive their BMW cars through red traffic lights while arguing with their stockbrokers on their mobile phones. The concepts of the complex landscape and of co-evolution should remind managers that firms are interconnected in many strange ways. The simple model of competition, each for himself and the devil take the hindmost, is a pretty poor model of any society, but a hopelessly inadequate one of an economy in which growth and innovation are occurring.

Firms that are nominally engaged in fierce competition may be, in effect, cooperating to expand their common market and improve their common operating technology. At the same time a firm that neither of them have heard of may be plotting an innovation that will eventually lead to their utter destruction.

Leaping into the unknown

Evolutionary leaps are generally involuntary, and mostly fatal. In nature they require changes amounting to a major mutation, leading a recognisably different species. Stephen Jay Gould suggested that the required changes could occur in one, or in very few, generations and called the resulting creatures "hopeful monsters". Rather than leading their established species to a generally higher level of evolutionary fitness, such hopeful monsters are, in Gould's "punctuated equilibrium" model, the founding members of a new species.

Not all biologists believe that all, or even any, new species start with major mutations. When environmental changes, climatic or geological, take place the members of a species may be separated into two non-communicating niches. Since the environmental pressures in the two niches are likely to differ, the members of the species in each will start an adaptive walk up a new mountain. After a million or so years of separate evolution the two groups may be so distinct as to be unable to interbreed: they will have evolved into new species.

The unit of economic evolution is the firm, including in that term the millions of hopeful inventors toiling in their garages around the world to create the next internal combustion engine, aeroplane or computer. Judging by the patent statistics, there are hundreds or even thousands of inventions for every new product that makes it to the market, and even making it to the market does not establish a product's long term success. Many new products are withdrawn after a while with no successors: the Stanley Steamer is as extinct as the dodo.

Firms have, of course, a life of their own. Even when an inventor creates the basis for a genuinely new class of products there is no guarantee that the inventor will still be around when the product becomes a success on the market. Even the initial firm's identity is often lost as the result of a takeover or its eviction from the market by a successful "fast follower". A few pioneers enjoy lasting fame and success, but more of them enjoy no more than the posthumous fame of being the first person to find the trail and the first occupant of the graveyard at the end of it.

It is useful, for a moment, to focus on the "metafirm", a hypothetical entity that came into existence at the moment an inventor decided to work on the solution to some problem. The metafirm includes all the people who will become involved with the invention between the time of its conception and the time it becomes a mature, profitable enterprise. The metafirm undertakes the journey from one mountain peak, into the

Darwin's finches

In 1831 the young Charles Darwin was engaged as a naturalist to travel on HMS Beagle as it undertook a scientifically oriented circumnavigation. In the Galapagos Islands, off the coast of Ecuador, he observed that a unique form of tortoise, mockingbird, and finch inhabited each island; the various forms differed in structure and eating habits from island to island. Their similarities suggested that they were closely related, but their differences were those expected of remote cousins rather than siblings.

Darwin struggled to find a rational explanation for these differences, eventually coming to the theory of evolution as a result of natural selection. Rising sea levels (or sinking land) had created geographic barriers between what had been members of a single group of species, and the subtle differences in each of the new environments led to substantial differences between the different groups of descendants.

valleys, and blunders through the chaotic fog until it finds the foothills of a new mountain range. Only once the new mountain has been conquered is the metafirm a success and the new product established.

History belongs to the victors, and once a new firm is established and the trail to the new mountain blazed it is easy to forget the many concepts that never made it, the metafirms that vanished into the fog, or those that conquered fearful barriers only to find that their new mountain was no higher than the one that they had left. A century after their era ended we can look back on the cable tram as an amusing Victorian folly and San Francisco tourist attraction, but we should spare a thought for the American engineers and entrepreneurs who perfected cable tram technology less than two years before the first successful demonstration of an electric tramway. The cable tramway entrepreneurs found a new mountain, but long before they could enjoy the fruits of their efforts another group of climbers emerged on a higher mountain still.

The innovating enterprise

The metafirm concept provides some interesting insights into the innovation process. The point of struggling to the top of a mountain in the first place is that the firms that reach the peak survive, which in the commercial world means achieving a competitive return on the capital employed. If the firm sends one or more of its members to explore the valleys around in the hope of finding the path up a new mountain, or in more conventional language, attempts a major innovation, these members need to be supported during their excursion. An R&D department, in other words, must be supported out of the recurrent operations of the firm since, whatever its future prospects, it cannot generate the *current* revenue needed to feed and clothe its members and their families.

In subsistence economies innovation becomes difficult or impossible simply because the slack needed to support the innovator is not there. An inventor might propose the use of bows and arrows to hunters familiar with spears and traps, but the hunters of her tribe must accept the risk that bows and arrows will be less successful than the traditional hunting techniques before they can experiment with them. Since they will have perfected their use of spears and traps and have little experience of using bows and arrows their first few hunts with the new weapon are very likely to be less successful than they would have been with the older ones. The consequences of the failure of a hunting innovation in a subsistence community are not embarrassment or monetary loss, but the real possibility that the hunt will fail and the hunters' families will starve. Incremental evolution will flourish under subsistence conditions, at least until the evolutionary catastrophe is reached, but radical innovation will be extremely rare.

Even in the nominally developed world the cost of searching for new innovations is widely regarded as a severe drain on the public welfare. In Australia, before 1997, the government, through the R&D tax concession and the R&D syndication scheme, contributed about 0.5 per cent of Australia's GDP to the support of innovation. The incoming government, claiming a mandate for "fiscal responsibility", declared that this level of support was not affordable and slashed it by 60 per cent. The private sector responded to this initiative by cutting its own R&D expenditure, and for the first time in fifteen years the amount Australian firms invested in innovation started to fall.

Innovation is expensive in time as well as in equipment, and the innovators and their families must be supported while they search for new opportunities and are distracted from extracting value from current ones. The limitations on this support set the limit on the ambitions of would-be innovators.

There is quite a close analogy between exploration and innovation. English society had become relatively prosperous by the late eighteenth century, prosperous enough to send Captain Cook and the barque

Endeavour on a two year voyage of discovery. The motives of the Admiralty and the English government were not purely scientific, and they certainly hoped that Cook would make useful discoveries; but Cook was not expected to turn a profit on the voyage itself. This may be compared with the preceding English circumnavigation, by Drake two hundred years earlier. Science and exploration played little role in Drake's plans; he was engaged on a commercially successful pirate voyage, and he circumnavigated as the only way to get home without running the gauntlet of the aroused and angry Spanish fleet that was waiting for him on the more direct route.

Two hundred years after Captain Cook's voyages the US placed men on the moon in a project that would have been beyond the resources of any other government on earth or in history, and could not have been undertaken by any conceivable privately funded organisation.

Blackwell and Eilon, without referring to Kauffman's landscapes, were also interested in the relationship between the size of the sponsoring organisation and the ambition of the innovations which it underwrote.[2] They give a sympathetic account of the failure of Rolls-Royce in 1971, as it struggled to complete the triple-shaft RB211 jet engine. Rolls-Royce had been pushed into agreeing to the development by the Wilson labour government, but in 1971 the Heath conservative government was in power and they were less sympathetic to industry policy initiatives. By a stroke of irony the free-market conservatives were forced to nationalise the insolvent Rolls-Royce and supervise the completion of the RB211 contract.

Rolls-Royce had discovered a new mountain, but their resources ran out before they were able to conquer it. Once they were taken over by the British government the resource constraint was lifted the RB211 became a major commercial success. Rolls-Royce was eventually re-privatised by Mrs Thatcher's conservative government.

Percolation and the edge of chaos

Kauffman also investigated a different, but related model, based on logical networks rather than fitness landscapes. Each network contains a large number of elements, each of which responds, on a regular basis, to the state of one or more other elements according to logical rules. Evolution, or attempted innovation, is simulated by making arbitrary changes to the state of some of the network nodes or the rules connecting them. The concept seems remarkably like a computer put together by thousands of mentally challenged monkeys, but Kauffman was nevertheless able to deduce some important laws of organisation by analysing the concept.

One of Kauffman's results is that this random computer will settle down to a very small subset of all the possible states, and under plausible conditions most of these will be either stable or short period oscillations. There will still be some long-period or chaotic attractors affecting part of the network. Even a system apparently designed to maximise disorder produces a great deal of order. There are a few chaotic oceans in a world of stability and predictability.

If such a system is repeatedly perturbed, as an ecology might be by further mutations or an economy by repeated attempts to innovate, the general pattern of large regions of stability or predictability interpenetrated by regions of chaotic unpredictability remains, but the locations of the zones change. The edges of some of the chaotic oceans freeze while elsewhere regions that were solid begin to melt. Depending on one's perspective, the stable regions percolate through the chaotic ones or vice versa.

When this model is applied to a real ecology or economy, the image that emerges is of evolution "at the edge of chaos". At the boundary between the frozen land and chaotic ocean change is possible and there is sufficient short term predictability to sift beneficial mutations, or innovations, from the others and incorporate them into the stable zone. On the frozen land, change is impossible, while in the middle of the chaotic oceans all semblance of cause and effect is lost and there is no way to separate beneficial from other mutations and innovations.

Kauffman suggests that, in nature, the evolutionary process has itself evolved to keep living organisms close to the edge of chaos. The most successful human organisations and societies may well have evolved, in their culture, their expectations, and their patterns of acceptable behaviour, to stay on the edge of chaos too.

Economics

The orthodox neoclassical school of economics, building on the work of Walras, Jevons and Pareto and dominant today, takes as its fundamental assumption the view that a market economy is, or would be if governments, large companies and trade unions were abolished, in the most perfect achievable social and economic state. The obvious current problems faced by all real economies and societies are dismissed by reference to the "long run" when a state of perfect equilibrium will be reached. In Kauffman's terminology, the neoclassical school of

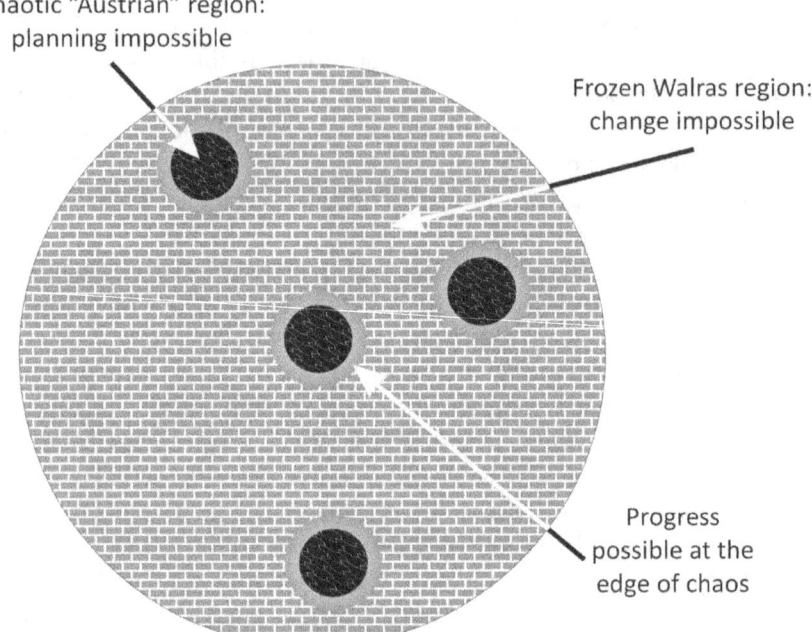

Chaotic "Austrian" region: planning impossible

Frozen Walras region: change impossible

Progress possible at the edge of chaos

Figure 7.1   The edge of chaos

Every point within the circle represents a possible state of a living species or human organisation. From many points a disturbance will have no lasting effect and the status quo will return more or less rapidly. From other points a disturbance, however small, will have a major and unpredictable effect. At the boundary between the frozen and chaotic regions valuable changes can be captured and preserved. Kauffman called this the edge of chaos.

economics limits its field of study to the frozen region of the space of economic possibilities.

The neoclassical school self-destructed, as far as any claim to real-world applicability was concerned, when Arrow and Debreu set out the necessary conditions for a perfect equilibrium state. These are, in essence, that at some point in time every economic agent (household or firm) makes a proposal as to what they will make or consume as every point in time from then to infinity. An "auctioneer" then checks to see that all these proposals are consistent, and if they are not, requires agents to adjust their expectations until they are.

Once all the agents' plans are consistent the auctioneer retires and everybody then follows their plan until the end of time. An economic theory that relied on the assumption that no one could invent anything new, or even change their mind, or have an accident, lacked credibility.

Robert Lucas[3] from the University of Chicago, came to the rescue of the equilibrium model with his concept of "rational expectations". Lucas argued that since people were rational they would observe the results of their own and other people's past behaviour and adjust their own future behaviour to avoid actions that led to trouble and reinforce those that turned out well. By taking this approach (and by making numerous other assumptions of either doubtful or negligible relevance to the real world) Lucas claimed to be able to show that the economy and therefore a society, to the extent that economists distinguish between them, would progress to a perfect equilibrium even without an auctioneer.

Equilibrium theories, plain or fancy, have a number of attractions for neoliberal economists (known in Australia as "economic rationalists") and their political disciples. One of these is the explanation that they offer for poverty and unemployment. In the plain theory, if someone is unemployed or poor it is because they, or their ancestors, chose to be so when all the economic decisions were made under the eye of the auctioneer. In the fancy rational expectations version, people who are poor or unemployed are so because they are insufficiently rational to make the correct choices in the market of life, and so are beyond help. Either way, governments that try to alleviate poverty or unemployment can only do so at the expense of the rest of society. The religious men who passed by the victim of violent robbery, in the parable of the Good Samaritan, were economically rational, while the Good Samaritan, in the economically rational version of the parable, was a busybody who preserved the life of one whom the economy had rejected.

Chaos and complexity theory have erected at least two insuperable barriers to the applicability of rational expectations theory to the real world. One springs from the nature of a complex landscape (see above), and the other from deterministic chaos. Because real-world effects have multiple causes and the value of various outcomes depend on combinations of single process outcomes, there are a large number of separate local maximum points to which an economy can converge. If economic agents are restricted to local or bounded rationality (that is, whatever the quality of their reasoning powers they must rely on limited information) it becomes highly probable (for practical purposes certain) that the economy will approach a local optimum which is, on whatever measures may be adopted, much less desirable than the global optimum state. The achievement of the global optimum requires people to be "hyper-rational", capable of instantaneously solving equations that a computer the size of the universe could not have made a dent in since the dawn of time.

Hyper-rationality is so improbable that the original idea of the auctioneer and the elimination of time seems almost reasonable. Chaos theory offers a second, but clearly related, barrier to the rational expectations hypothesis. Because most real life phenomena of economic and social interest depend, to some extent, on their antecedents, and practically all relationships between phenomena are non-linear, the phenomenon of sensitivity to initial conditions is omnipresent. Observing the past does *not* provide an infallible guide to future conduct, because events too insignificant to notice (like the butterfly in the Amazon forest) can lead to radically different outcomes. Drawing sufficient correct lessons from history to provide a guide to future conduct requires infinitely precise omniscience, the ability to measure, not to many decimal places, but to an infinite number of decimal places. This is no more realistic than the assumption of hyper rationality, and yet the theory of rational expectations requires *both* assumptions.

The Chicago school

The most extreme devotees of the neoclassical model of an economy are associated with the University of Chicago and its fan club in the Royal Bank of Sweden. The members of the Chicago School eliminate, by definition, any form of imperfect competition or market power except where sustained by the activities of governments. This gives their recommendations a libertarian twist, since they share the Austrian school's distaste for governments and trade unions (but not for large companies).

Followers of the Chicago School may be distinguished from the Austrian school by their Panglossian claim that the economy is in the best possible state, or would be if governments restricted their interventions to the suppression of trade unions. The Austrians deny that the economy is in an optimal state, that anyone could describe such a state, or even that there could be any systematic way of organising a society or an economy so as to progress to such a state.

The late Milton Friedman was one of the chief glories of the Chicago School, although his neoclassicism often appears to have a distinctly "Austrian" colouring. Friedman attempted to define the minimum function of government consistent with Hayek's assertion that no action by government could increase the general welfare.

Friedman developed the doctrine of monetarism, which defined the optimum role of government as to control the money supply according to rules Friedman thoughtfully set out, and to leave everything else to the market. Friedman's policies were adopted by the UK government under Mrs (now Baroness) Thatcher in 1979 and by the US Government of Ronald Reagan in 1981. The effect in both countries was disastrous and both governments abandoned the experiment in 1983. This has not prevented Friedman's elevation to cult status among neoliberal economists and far right lobbyists.

The Austrians

The "Austrian" school of economics is generally associated with Frederich Hayek, and Ludwig von Mises. Their influence is also felt in the "public choice" school of economists. The starting point of Austrian theory is familiar to students of chaos generally: in a complex system, such as an economy, the number and degree of linkages between the various components is such that the long term effect of any manipulation of any single component is all but unpredictable.

The Austrians, or at least von Mises, also struck upon the fundamental logical point that the application of a statistical process to data concerning a population necessarily eliminates the effect of individual contributions: that the legitimacy of proceeding from data about individuals into an aggregate or average concerning a group of individuals, the reverse procedure is logically impermissible: knowledge of the average properties of members of a population says almost nothing about the properties of any individual member of that population, and the larger the population, the less valid is the application of statistical averages to any single member of it.

The distinctive characteristic of the Austrian school is the assumption that because the effect of any action undertaken by a government cannot be quantified precisely in advance, governments should undertake no actions with an economic consequence or an economic purpose. This has become a serious limitation on the influence of the Austrian School: if their only practical advice is "do nothing", governments need to employ very few economists to say so. Ambitious economics students might seek instruction in a variant of the discipline with greater employment opportunities.

Von Mises and his follower Hayek anticipated some of the results of modern chaos theory, including the complexity and fundamental unpredictability of the real world. This led them to ridicule general equilibrium theory. Hayek developed this insight into a general critique of state involvement in the economy, on the ground that an economy's intrinsic unpredictability made it impossible to demonstrate that such an intervention did more harm than good.

The most ardent followers of von Mises now denounce Hayek for his supposed compromises with the neoclassical school, but the distinctions drawn are hard for outsiders to appreciate.

Chaos and complexity theories suggest two main critiques of the Hayek and Friedman positions. Since chaos is deterministic, it becomes possible for governments and other economic agents to make short term plans with a reasonable prospect of success. Medium and long term success requires active management, progressing one step at a time, but it is by no means impossible. In a deeply chaotic state, of course, the predictive horizon might be so short that even active management could not make progress; but complex systems generally exhibit stable as well as chaotic regions, and progress becomes possible at the "edge of chaos".

Malthus and the Law of Proportion

Thomas Malthus is most widely known for his gloomy prediction that the human population would grow to the point that the food supply was exhausted and so the natural state of the majority of humanity was destitution. Economic historians also know him for his contribution to the development of classical economics along with Smith and Ricardo and for the inspiration that part of his work offered to J M Keynes. One relatively neglected aspect of Malthus's work was his Law of Proportions.[4]

Malthus observed that many real phenomena were, in modern terminology, over-determined; they had multiple causes, all of which must be present but no single one of which could legitimately be described as the sole or even primary cause. Naïve observers might regard the most recent of the causes to appear as *the* cause, but experiment and observation would often show that this appearance was only accidental. Had the various causes appeared in a different order some other one would have appeared to have been decisive. Malthus was also well aware of the possibility of both positive and negative feedback (to apply modern terms to his concepts) and the consequent possibility that there could be "too much of a good thing". Land reform might be desirable if large, ill-managed estates were divided between efficient yeoman farmers, but if the process were carried too far the result would be inefficient peasant agriculture.

Malthus's Law of Proportion required that the various forces acting on an economy be kept in balance. Only fanatics would, in his view, argue that any single aspect of economic behaviour was so important that it should be pursued regardless of all other considerations. One suspects that a reborn Malthus would be contemptuous of those who in modern times see one solution to every problem, whether they propose microeconomic reform or official intervention.

Malthus observed that every economic decision required at least two causes: someone needed both the *power* and the *will* to implement it. A manufacturer might have the will to expand, but lack the money; while a banker might have the power to lend the money the manufacturer needed, but be unwilling to do so. Action only occurred when the power and the will coincided. A similar modern dichotomy separates those economists who advocate supply side reforms and those who wish to undertake demand management measures. The supply-siders argue that businesses must be given access to cheap and readily accessible services, raw materials and components so as to encourage investment; while the demand managers assert that no business will invest unless it foresees an adequate level of demand for the goods and services that the investment could produce. Supply-siders emphasize the power while demand managers emphasise the will; and representatives of the two factions abuse each other in language which at times makes the proverbial fishwife seem refined. They are, of course, both right and both wrong. Since 1970 the supply-siders have dominated both the economics profession and the production of intemperate and arrogant assessments of those who disagree with them.

It is not very surprising that a learned Anglican divine, as Malthus was, should emphasise moderation. The Church of England defined itself as steering the middle path between the "superstition" of the Roman Catholic Church and the dogma and intolerance of the Calvinists and Presbyterians. The partisans of both extreme positions may abuse the man in the middle; Malthus was frequently accused of being unable to make up his mind.

From Malthus to Kauffman

The concept of the edge of chaos brings us back very close to Malthus's Law of Proportion. If our society and economy has become frozen, sterile, immobile then it is correct to push towards the ocean of chaos: the call must be to deregulate, break down structural rigidities, encourage competition. If, on the other hand, society and the economy are drowning in the chaotic ocean then one must swim towards the frozen shore: regulate, control, impose structure, relax pro-competitive policies.

The great defect of human nature seems to be a combination of herd effects and a tendency to linear thinking. If some reform has proved beneficial, then too many people fall into the trap of thinking that more reform must be even better. While the Soviet Union may now be seen as little more than an unpleasant part of history, it might be useful to remember that in 1922 Lenin's successful New Economic Policy introduced a mixed economy with the major utilities and arsenals under state control but much of the economy in private hands. A dispassionate observer (not that anyone was dispassionate about the Russian Revolution in the 1920s) might have found it hard to distinguish Lenin's policy from Chamberlain's "municipal socialism" that had given the English city of Birmingham sewerage, tramways and a gas supply by the start of the twentieth century.

Lenin had spent many years as an exile in Switzerland, and it is hardly surprising that he came to admire the Swiss combination of socially responsible municipal government and civilised capitalism. It was Lenin's successor, the paranoid and xenophobic Stalin, who decided that if some state control was good, more was better. Stalin reversed the NEP, instituting rigid state control over every sector of the economy at a huge cost in life and with the ultimate result of utter economic stagnation.

When the moderate Gorbachev attempted to thaw the Soviet economy in the 1980s with policies of *perestroika* and *glasnost* he was thrust aside by the ebullient Yeltsin and his team of young economists. If slow perestroika was good, they argued, then fast perestroika must be better. If Mrs Thatcher had persuaded Gorbachev that it would take twenty five years to turn Russia into a modern economy they would show her what radical reform actually meant and do it in six months. It may be argued that Thatcher and Gorbachev were being too cautious, but history can't be restarted to find out. What is certain is that the policies of instant reform, or "shock therapy", all but killed the patient. By the end of the twentieth century the Russian economy was in a state of true chaos, and the number of people driven to a premature death by the changes was comparable to the cost of Stalin's collectivisation program.

Endnotes

1. Kauffman, Stuart A. (1993), *The Origins of Order: self-organisation and selection in evolution*, New York: Oxford University Press.

2. Blackwell, Basil & Eilon, Samuel (1991), *The Global Challenge of Innovation*, Oxford: Butterworth–Heinemann.

3. Lucas was the recipient of a Nobel Memorial Prize in Economics. Alfred Nobel was too good a business man to give any serious credence to economics and so his will made no provision for a prize in that discipline. The Royal Bank of Sweden founded the Nobel Memorial Prize in Economics as part of its domestic political agenda, and for several years made a point of awarding prizes to members of the Faculty of Economics of the University of Chicago to the practical exclusion of members most other economics schools. "Monetarism", an economic dogma championed by the Chicago school of economics exalts the role of central banks and demands that they be made independent of government.

4. Pullen, J. M. (1982), "Malthus on the doctrine of proportions and the concept of the optimum", *Australian Economic Papers* **2**1(39), pp. 270 – 85.

8. Taking Advantage

Conclusions

THE MOST BASIC conclusion that any book on chaos and business planning must arrive at is that Murphy's Law needs a new corollary. Murphy's Law states that: "Everything that can go wrong, will go wrong". O'Toole's corollary ("Murphy was an optimist") can now be refined: "Unexpected events will occur far more frequently than simple statistical laws imply".

Murphy and O'Toole remind engineers to leave nothing to chance. Don't assume anything. The planner is not in full control of events. The plans must assume certain patterns of behaviour by the business's customers, suppliers, competitors and regulators, and *all of these assumptions are more or less invalid.* The business planner should not rely on the assumption that the customers, competitors, suppliers and regulators are even going to act rationally according to any rules that the planner understands.

The planner can make a guess as to the most probable behaviour by the members of any of these groups, but must not underestimate the possibility of the improbable occurring. The planner can take some consolation that the planner's business, viewed from the outside, will not appear perfectly predictable either. Above all, the planner, the manager and the marketeer must think, watch and *adapt.*

Chaos and management

Chaos theory can begin to do for managers and marketeers what it is already doing for engineers. It can help set limits on the practical, to assess the risk level of policy proposals and to identify high risk areas. Chaos theory can help to puncture pompous pontificators: anybody who claims to know all the answers is mathematically certain to be at least partly wrong, and very likely to be wholly wrong. Even if, by some extraordinary stroke of luck, someone knew all the answers yesterday, most of them would be wrong by tomorrow.

Each individual can be shown by chaos theory to have a unique role to play: an individual does not often know what the final effects of his or her actions will be, but does know that they will have a real effect. The individual need not be submerged in a statistical mass. The small and medium business can survive and grow in direct competition with large businesses, contrary to some of the more gloomy implications of linear marketing theory. It will not necessarily be easy, but chaos theory shows that it is neither impossible nor arbitrarily difficult.

Chaos theory emphasises the role of luck. The self made man is, above all, the *lucky* man. The business that becomes the market leader in a new market will need to have been well managed and to have produced a sound range of products. Other businesses that occupy also-ran positions on the market share ladder may have been equally well managed and had equally good products. The market leader that *stays* on top will have senior managers with enough humility to recognise the role of luck or the hand of God. They will avoid confusing themselves with the Almighty.

Some senior managers lack this humility. They believe that the success that their business achieved was entirely a result of their own efforts. They may maintain this belief when the business had been large and successful before they were born. Such men will refuse to revise policies or to brook contradiction. They will turn their company into a mindless dinosaur. When they do take action, it will have no recognisable effect in progressing any legitimate business aim.

Senior employees of banks sometimes appear to believe that the size of their intellect is related to the size of the assets under their bank's control. Promotion to the top levels of the public service is also seen by some holders of exalted positions as a confirmation of their outstanding general ability.

Chaos theory suggests that some businesses may have market positions so impregnable that high levels of management incompetence will not cause any noticeable impact on their profits or market share in the short or medium term. The incompetence becomes exposed when they attempt to diversify into a growth area: after faffing about for a while they write off some staggering sum of money and announce that they are going to "concentrate on the core business". Concentrating on the core business may in fact mean retreating to a market where their decisions have practically no effect at all.

The managers of large companies supplying consumer commodities, like retail banking services, beer or petrol, are seldom aware of the chaotic properties of all markets. This may be because chaotic behaviour at the individual consumer level takes a long time to translate into large scale changes in their business operations. The severity of an event is measured by the time it takes as well as its magnitude.

A business that lost half its customers in a year would have experienced a catastrophic event. A business that suffered the same loss

American big oil thinks small

Most of the American oil industry still consists of fragments of Standard Oil, the vast combine established by John D Rockefeller in the 1880s and "trust busted" in 1909. John D Rockefeller played a major individual role in establishing Standard Oil and seeing the American oil industry through its establishment phase. By 1905 Henry Ford had begun making cars and it took little foresight to see the developing mass market in petrol consuming motor cars.

The nominally independent fragments of Standard Oil continued to operate in effective harmony for a further fifty years: outside the United States they did not maintain even the pretence of competition. By the late 1970s the senior managers of at least one of the fragments decided that their huge cash flows, ever-increasing profits and the attentions of ever more obsequious governments proved that they were superior to common men.

They decided to enter high technology, notably the office automation business. Since their profits and their top executive salaries were even higher than IBM's, they announced that they must be cleverer than IBM's managers and would shortly take over the number one spot in the computer industry. The oil company started by buying a promising office equipment supplier, and for a while things seemed to be going well. Suddenly the senior managers of the oil major realised that further success in the office automation business would require new products: instead of spending the profits, they were going to have to make further investments.

They wrote off the office automation business in horror, and several hundred million dollars with it, and announced that they were "concentrating on their core business".

over thirty years might not notice any change at all.

Either event could be a result of chaos, in the sense that no person, even one with complete access to every source of relevant information and a fantastically powerful computer, could have predicted it. Some systems simply operate on longer time-scales than others.

Stable and less stable businesses

The most stable forms of business are those that supply frequently consumed products and services to individual consumers. Consumers in such markets do not change their preferences or their consumption patterns rapidly, and excessive management activity by a business supplying them is likely to be counter-productive. Because of the size of these markets, and the undemanding tasks involved in managing firms supplying them, these industries tend to be dominated by very large companies. This fact makes these markets somewhat risky for a small or medium company, since large, badly managed companies cannot be relied upon to act rationally.

Where a small or medium business has the opportunity to build a directly loyal customer base and a recognisable brand, the size and erratic behaviour of its larger competitors is likely to be less of a worry.

Businesses that supply consumer durable markets also tend to be large, and find that their markets are rather less forgiving and less stable. The management of such businesses cannot afford to be too erratic or unfocussed, since management and marketing mistakes can leave openings which competitors can exploit effectively. Such businesses should be considered one degree less stable than the suppliers of consumed consumer products, in that they require rational and consistent managing in order to survive and prosper.

Businesses that supply other businesses are in a substantially less stable situation still, because of the fact that their survival as a business depends on relatively few customers. Just how few depends on a number of factors. A business supplying undifferentiated large businesses in a single country, or small and medium businesses operating in a single region, would probably find that no more than thirty, and usually a lot fewer, clients would account for 80% of its business.

The most stable business to business firms are those supplying essential equipment used by small and medium businesses across a wide geographic area encompassing a number of economic regions. Such a business would be less affected than most by the sand pile effect. OfficeWorks in Australia or Staples in the USA serve this type of market. As many as 70% of its customers might need to be counted before 80% of the total business revenue is reached. The advantage of high stability would have been gained at the cost of managing a large number of relatively low value clients.

The least stable businesses are those supplying other businesses operating in a single industry within a single country or region. In many such cases these businesses will be dependent on less than four customers; there will be few with as many as fifteen major accounts. In either case these customers are likely to know each other, to talk about their suppliers, and to see each other's experience as directly relevant to their own business requirements. In such an industry bad news travels fast.

A business that is in a vulnerable position must consider whether it wants to do anything about it. If it is confident that its products are, and will remain, superior to any possible alternatives, and that its client relationships are, and will remain, strong, then the vulnerability is more apparent than real. A less confident business could consider reducing its dependence on such a small client base. Two possible approaches are product and geographic dispersion.

A business can develop, or acquire, an extension to its range of products that will allow it to start developing a customer base in an industry that has a similar pattern of requirements, but where the new industry sees itself as distinct from the industry that made up the business's original market. This is a base-replication strategy. The businesses that adopt this strategy will rely upon the restricted communication between its two customer bases to provide the required stability. Even where the products that are being sold are physically very similar, the different groups of customers will see the use that they are putting the products to as different.

The base replication approach requires the business to build a customer base in other countries and in other regions. Initially, this is likely to lead to greater stability, as inter-regional and international barriers restrict the extent to which the business's customers communicate. As the geographic strategy matures, it will move back towards the riskier posture of dependence but on a new national or international scale. A restricted number of customers will again account for over 80% of the business, but at least they will be much larger customers of a much larger business.

It is well known that there are risks and difficulties involved in expanding a business's markets into new regions and new countries. What is not generally realised is the magnitude of the risks involved for many businesses if they remain within a single region or country. Small and medium businesses are indeed "caught between the Devil and the deep blue sea". The sea can be sailed across: managing the Devil at close quarters may be rather more difficult.

Watch your rank

Exponents of conventional marketing strategy advise businesses to guard their market share. This is certainly the correct strategy for businesses supplying most frequently purchased consumer products.

Accountants and bank managers sometimes suggest that businesses should plan to achieve particular revenue levels. Such plans ignore the fact that a business's revenue levels depend upon the willingness of its customers to spend money in its markets. Since the eagerness of customers to spend money fluctuates, there is only one way an ordinary business can be sure of meeting revenue targets. This is to set them *too low*. This will automatically lead to the slackening of the business's marketing efforts as the targets are approached: everyone relaxes to some extent when the target is in sight. Such a business will slowly extinguish itself.

In industrial and consumer durable markets, a business's current market share may be hard to measure. One reason for this is that the business only has accurate data about its own revenue and must guess the revenue of the other businesses operating in its markets. Another is that firms, or households buying durable goods and infrequently needed services, may be a given firm's loyal customers even though circumstances prevent them from making any large purchases in the course of any one year. Furthermore, the relationship between market share and marketing effort is anything but straightforward in markets in complex products. Rather than using market share as a measure of the success of marketing and strategic development policies, a business can measure its rank.

Rank order is a single, definite number and one which will clearly differentiate businesses operating in the same market. A strategic objective stated in terms of holding rank, or gaining a certain number of places over a defined period, or entering a new market and gaining a particular rank, is definitively measurable. A general change in economic circumstances will affect all businesses operating in any particular market. If the change is a favourable one, businesses managed by revenue may indulge in an orgy of self congratulation, and businesses managed by market share may deduce (incorrectly) that their rising sales prove that their strategy is working.

Businesses managed by rank will measure the number of customers that they have, and the relative importance of customers that they have won and lost to their competition. These measures will accurately reflect the success of the business's marketing strategy, since uncontrollable economic effects will not affect the measurement.

General Electric, the US conglomerate with a major presence in white goods, medical electronics, aerospace, and financial services became, under its chairman Jack Welch, one of the most admired as well as the most profitable and valuable US corporations. GE's strictly enforced rule is that it will only enter industries where it expects to become the largest or second largest participant, and will exit any industries where it is not in one of the first two slots and has no realistic prospect of advancing to occupy one.

If it ain't broke ...

... don't fix it.

However a business has been managed up until the present time, and whatever the products and marketing tactics that have been used, the business will hold some rank in its markets. It will have a given market share and a given level of revenue. It will have competitors, and in some markets a given business's competitors will appear to be relatively successful.

There is no human structure that is beyond improvement, and the managers of most businesses will be well aware of possible improvements to their own business and its way of doing things. This creates a temptation to instigate changes in order to do better. Sometimes a business will appear to be in clear need of change: it may find itself losing large customers and with them its industry ranking and most if not all of its profits. Sometimes the stimulus to change will be that the business is quite successful, and wishes to become even more so. Before leaping on a metaphorical horse and galloping off madly in all directions, the business must take a dispassionate look at where it is and why. The forces that hold a business to its rank in its industry are relatively weak, and the forces that prevent it rising further are relatively strong.

Progress involves risk; because change occurs at the edge of chaos the full consequences of any decision cannot be known in advance. Since a market economy is normally growing and changing, a firm that does not change will go into a relative decline at least, and probably an absolute decline as its customers and rivals make changes of their own. If a firm is sufficiently far from the edge of chaos small changes and initiatives will have no lasting effects, and larger and more dangerous ones may become essential.

Radical changes, particularly those that place major customer relationships at risk, are extremely hazardous. Like medical heroics, sudden radical change should be restricted to patients on the point of death in any case. If the effect of such changes is to cause the business's major customers to doubt the usefulness of the supplier relationship, the risk of a disastrous revenue collapse rises by a factor of seven. If a

Govett's Leap

An English-based high technology company examined its customer base, and discovered that about fifty customers accounted for over 70% of its revenue. They did some, but not all, of the sums described in this book and realised their apparent vulnerability.

A proposal was raised to abandon the dangerous pursuit of large customers and to build a secure mass market among the small ones by a radical restructuring of the company's product portfolio, its investment strategy, and its marketing approach. In its home market, the strategy was abandoned at the first test, when the largest single customer responded to news of it by transferring the equipment order for a huge project to the English company's major competitor.

The Australian subsidiary of the English company was not shaken in its resolve, and vigorously pursued the new policy. The defection of a few major customers was not seen as a reason to abandon the strategy, which was pursued until 75% of the company's major customers had deserted it. The strategic re-positioning had been achieved without loss of market share: from 10% of the *whole* market the subsidiary now held 10% of the smallest 25% of the market (by value). The subsidiary's rank in the Australian market dropped from 2nd to 20th, but rank was not among the measurement criteria the English company employed.

The senior manager who had supervised this triumph was recalled to England and promoted.

business is not in a state of near terminal collapse, then change should be gradual, building upon what the business already has, and above all, maintaining the confidence of the business's major customers.

Games people play

The favourite games in a particular culture give an insight into the type of thinking that is encouraged in such a society. The thinking, in turn, will lead to models of "proper" behaviour and the development of theories that justify such behaviour.

Poker

Poker is a quintessentially American game. It is statistically fair, so that the outcome of a game played between players of similar skill starting with equal stakes using an unmarked, shuffled pack cannot be predicted. Three major elements of poker stand out when using it as a strategic planning model.

Poker is a game of bluff and secrecy: it is important that a player's opponents do not know what her current holding is.

Poker is a gambling game with a built-in martingale: players must be prepared to place relatively large sums at risk in order to retain a chance of winning, and a player in a winning position can be defeated by running out of money.

Poker is a game of power: there are weak hands, strong hands and invincible hands. In most versions of poker the players have an opportunity to strengthen their hands by shrewd play.

A culture which understands poker would understand the ideal point theory of marketing, and in particular the high investment that is justified when the ideal point is located: the player holding a full house in five card draw poker should not be bluffed into folding. From the 1890s until the middle 1970s the poker approach succeeded and American business appeared to be on the point of worldwide domination.

Go

The ancient Japanese game of *go* has little in common with poker. All moves in go are played in the open using simple stones of equal weight. No single move can have an immediate dramatic effect on a game, and outright defeat for a player (in the sense of being forced off the board) would be an unusual outcome. The objective of go is to capture territory by placing contiguous lines of stones, and games end by agreement at which point the winner is the player with the most territory.

Expert go players demonstrate amazing foresight by apparent random placements early in the game which will become the linchpin of a strategic ploy tens or hundreds of moves later. A businessman steeped in the philosophy of go would have no difficulty in comprehending the fractal market and the need to take a long term strategic view of it. He or she would expect to move from secure position to secure position. Opponents would not be defeated by force, but by subtlety. Victory would generally take the form of cooption, not destruction or enslavement.

The shock of defeat in the Second World War and the ensuing occupation prompted Japan to adopt a global strategy for its re-industrialisation. The "oil shocks" of 1973 and 1979 gave this strategy added importance, and during the 1980s Japanese manufacturing moved to clear world leadership of a number of industries.

The Americans proved largely incapable of responding to the Japanese challenge in manufacturing, but in the early 1990s they managed to change the rules of international competition by demanding, and getting, liberalisation of Japan's financial markets. Instead of rewarding companies and countries that made superior goods and delivered superior services, the rewards went to companies and countries where the share prices rose fastest.

The go-playing Japanese did not prove adept at financial poker, and Japan's economy slipped from growth to stagnation and recession.

Chess

Chess is a Russian game in the same degree as poker is American or go, Japanese. Chess is like go, in that all moves are in the open, and like poker, in that some pieces represent more power than others. It is like neither, in having a definition of victory. Games of go and poker end when the players give up or are sent broke. Chess ends in check-mate. Chess is a game derived from warfare.

Chess is not a game for business strategists. It would be a serious mistake to believe that the Russians who guided the former USSR's economy into a shambles were stupid, or alternatively that they actually intended to make such a mess.

Their whole way of thinking about management problems was wrong, and wrong habits of thinking lead to wrong answers. They attempted to find the right answer to every problem, and the effort took so long that by the time they uttered it, it was wrong.

The new international order

America's successful rewriting of the international rules disadvantaged Japan, where most companies operated off a small equity base and a substantial secured debt, usually owed to their *keiretsu* banking partner. Share prices in Japan at the end of the 1980s were very high relative to profits, and there was little room to move upwards. Japan's post-1975 tradition of consensus made its companies reluctant to get a quick profit boost by downsizing. Neither constraint affected the USA. Its major companies were moderately geared, and earnings per share could be raised by borrowing money from banks and from the bond market; this was assisted by the low interest rate policy of the US Federal Reserve Bank under Alan Greenspan.

Real chess

The Russian High Command always treated the Second World War as a complex chess problem. Even in the first few months of their participation in the war every move the Russians made had a strategic purpose. In autumn 1941, with the Russian front collapsing and the fall of Moscow apparently imminent, the Russians sent a delegation to Britain and America to discuss 1942 deliveries of machine tools.

By the beginning of 1944 it was clear that the German invasion of Russia had been a costly failure. It was not clear that an Allied invasion of Germany was going to be any more successful. The Russians started that year in a position of tactical parity with Germany and in particular without any realistic prospect of delivering a crippling blow at Germany proper.

Some British and American politicians believed that Russia should just hold its Western frontier and let the Western Allies defeat Germany after invading France and the Balkans. The Russians thought that this was militarily optimistic, and in any case it did not fit in with Russia's plans for the post war chess game. They sought and found a strategic solution.

In nine carefully orchestrated battles, the Russians teased and tormented the Germans until 130 of Germany's 165 divisions were on the flanks and too far from the main direction to intervene in the battle for the defence of the approaches to Germany. In the last months of 1944 the Russians launched the tenth battle, Operation Bagration, and seized the direct road to Berlin.

At the beginning of 1945 the Russians crashed through Poland to the gates of Berlin, and by May 2nd Hitler was dead and the Russians flag flew over the Reichstag. On May 9th the Russians celebrated their victory in the War, and began to lose the peace.

During the 1990s American companies engaged upon an orgy of downsizing and leveraged takeovers, all of them intended to increase the reported profit per share even though many of them shrank the revenue base from which the profit was earned and boosted the earnings per share by cunning manipulation of their balance sheets.

The rising profits forced the Dow-Jones index, a measure of average share prices, from just over 2000 to over 9000 during the decade. The shrinking productive capacity of the US economy led to rapidly rising trade deficits, but the capital flight from countries where profits were not rising at the US rate pushed the US dollar up when traditional trade theory claimed that it should have fallen.

Japan, whose high productivity industries generated large trade surpluses, saw its currency fall as investors took money out to buy US dollar assets. The flow of funds into the US pushed the US dollar higher and made US dollar assets look even more attractive to investors. Capital flight pushed Indonesia, Thailand and South Korea into a severe recession at the end of 1997 and did the same to Russia in mid 1998. Only the US economy continued to grow, riding a wave of "positive investor sentiment", something to be compared with the hot air that lifts balloons. By late 1998 not even hot air could keep the Dow Jones index rising, and since only the expectation of further rises had kept it up, it began to fall.

US stock prices overall did not fall with the Dow Jones index, since the running was picked up by an extraordinary boom in the share prices of high technology and Internet-related stocks. If exaggerated expectations had driven the Dow Jones' rise to 9000, words fail to give an account of some of the price gains for Internet-related stocks. By early 2000 there was an almost general consensus to the effect that the Internet boom was a bubble waiting to burst, and the valuations of several high technology stocks were nearly as suspect.

2001 saw the bursting of the tech bubble with some share prices dropping by more than fifty per cent in a few weeks; but instead of investing in real industry US banks and investors pumped money into the housing market, creating an even bigger bubble which collapsed in 2007, triggering a global financial crisis.[1]

The business strategist

In business there are no decisive victories. One opponent may be destroyed or taken over, but another will appear. A good chess mind would suit a competitive salesman: in a sales campaign there is an objective, and at the end of it there is a clear victory or a clear defeat. A salesman who gets promoted to a marketing or to a general management position needs to learn strategic subtlety, to think more of advantage and less of victory.

The Roman emperor Caligula is supposed to have regretted that the Roman people did not have a single neck, thereby depriving him of the pleasure of killing them all with one blow. The poker approach to business strategy suffers from the same problem: no market consists of people all of whom think the same, and no single stroke of guile or genius can propel a supplier to market domination. Occasionally a dramatic movement may be needed to preserve a company's position.

More often what is required is patient development, building on strength, reinforcing weakness, seizing proffered advantages and only gambling on favourable odds. Above all, as the Russian experience shows, a quick decision *might* be wrong, although in a chaotic market driven environment this may not ever become apparent. A delayed decision is almost certainly going to be wrong, because the information upon which it was based will no longer be correct.

In chess and war the clock or the enemy set a time limit on the possible delay in making and promulgating a decision. In a market economy, a business's competitors serve the same purpose. The market economy is unquestionably superior to the command economy by every measure except the ease with which a nation may be turned into an armed camp. This is true while practically all the explanations given by orthodox economists for the superiority of the market are demonstrably false or inconsistent with their own basic theories.[2]

The goad to decision making that the market economy provides, the automatic deletion of ditherers, may be the true key to the superiority of the market over the command economy as a basis for social organisation.

Endnotes

1   Stiglitz, Joseph (2010), *Freefall: Free markets and the sinking of the global economy*, London: Allen Lane.

2   Hunt, Shelby D. & Morgan, Robert M. (1995), "The Comparative Advantage Theory of Competition", *Journal of Marketing* **59**(April), pp. 1–15.

9. A Brief History of Chaology

Science and human affairs

FOR THREE HUNDRED years, since Galileo, Newton and Leibnitz[1] worked and wrote, there has been a "scientific" explanation of the world and its ways. This scientific explanation competes with the religious and mystical ones. This explanation compared the universe to a grandfather clock. The universe, thought Leibnitz, was as predictable as a well oiled clock, and just a little more complicated.[2] Leibnitz's successors, the philosophers of the eighteenth century Enlightenment, extended his confidence about the working of the universe to equally confident predictions about human affairs. In particular, the discipline of *political economy*[3] was invented at about this time.

The political economists held that need in human affairs had the same function as gravity in the universe, and that the market was the best way to ensure that needs were satisfied. Their successors to this day use the mathematics of Newton and Leibnitz to prove that the best solution to every human problem can be found in the untrammelled operation of a deregulated market.

A scientific explanation is tested by scientists by its predictive power: a good scientific theory can be tested by experiments. In fifteen exciting years between 1890 and 1905 Becquerel, Roentgen and Einstein[4] shattered the grandfather clock theory beyond repair. Over a hundred years of experience with political economy might have caused some doubt to creep in, but by and large economists have stuck to the results of their Newtonian mathematics and the advice of the eighteenth century philosophers.

After Einstein, before Chaos

Mainstream studies in physics tended to turn away from the world following the shocks administered by relativity and quantum theory. Physicists came to live out the caricature of the expert who knows more and more about less and less. PhD degrees are awarded in showers to workers who find out new facts about atomic particles so elusive that they only exist for a billionth of a second. At the other extreme, most cosmologists limited their studies of the universe to the first ten minutes after the Big Bang. Everything that happened in the fifteen billion or so years between the Big Bang and the present day was

Chaos — first, the bad news

Chaos, or a tendency to unpredictable behaviour, lurks in practically every real world system.

Sometimes it is hidden, only waiting to burst out and spread confusion.

Sometimes chaos is the normal operating state of a system.

regarded as too boring to worry about or too complicated to be worth trying to understand.

Real world events were generally left to the applied scientists and engineers, as needing a lot of boring calculation but containing nothing of "real" scientific interest. One of the few top rank theoreticians who took any interest in the real world was the Russian, Landau. Landau thought that a clock could be understood because it only had a few parts and a few connections between them. Complex real world objects, like running taps, were made up of billions upon billions of molecules with quadrillions and quadrillions of connections between them, and although they obeyed the same laws as a grandfather clock, their equations of motion would take the life of the universe to write out, much less solve.

In essence, Landau looked at complex systems, agreed that they were too complex to simplify into readily calculated mathematics, and went on to other subjects.

Economists continued to use the mathematics of Newton and Leibnitz, but they felt obliged to explain why their theories never seem to lead to accurate predictions. The explanation that they settled on was borrowed from electronic engineering. It is called noise. The economists continue to believe that the world really runs like a grandfather clock, in steady, predictable and calculable ways. It is just difficult to see what it is really doing at any one time. Errors in economic policy are caused, according to orthodox economic theory, by difficulties in measurement, not because the policies are based upon invalid assumptions.

It is only in the last few years that the tools developed by chaology have been applied to determining whether failures in economic policy are purely random (as suggested by classical economics) or have a systematic component (as suggested by chaos theory). The evidence strongly suggests chaotic, rather than random, behaviour.

The theory of chaos

It was all very well for Landau to write off the problems of the real world and direct his powerful intellect to other problems. Applied scientists and engineers had to cope with turbulence and other real world phenomena because that was their job. A meteorologist has not got the luxury of saying that clouds behave in unpredictable ways and giving forecasts qualified by the warning that "this forecast will only be correct if the weather is cloudless". An engineer would not be readily forgiven if the aircraft he designed fell out of the sky whenever they met turbulence in the air stream.

Economists have generally learned the trick of identifying the problems as part of their forecasting process: "everything will turn out rosy if everyone does the right thing and there are lots of micro-economic reforms". When things don't turn out quite as rosily as predicted it is usually possible to find some micro-economic reform that was not completed rapidly enough or with sufficient savagery to explain the error in the forecast.

A few applied scientists, engineers and a very few economists kept plugging away at the problems of complexity, and a small school of Russian mathematicians around Kolmogorov had never quite given up on the subject. By the mid 1980s the study of complex dynamic systems had rejoined the mainstream of physics and mathematics, and the fractured foundations of the neoclassical school of economics were becoming visible while the edifice still stood.

Chaology, or Dynamic Systems Theory, or Non-Linear Dynamics, is a new and respectable branch of mathematics. Mathematicians tend to give words a very specific meaning, and their use of the word "chaos" is no exception. To a mathematician, chaos is simply a state in which we cannot be certain just what is going to happen next, even on those occasions when we have a pretty good grasp of what is happening now. What has been discovered in the course of research into chaos theory is that many, and possibly most, examples of complicated behaviour can be explained by *relatively* few underlying relationships. Such behaviour is referred to as *Deterministic Chaos*.

Deterministic Chaos was initially used to describe theoretical systems where very simple, well understood objects obeying well understood physical laws do unpredictable, or "random" things. It has now been shown to apply to many real-world systems. Roulette provides a typical example of a highly engineered piece of machinery operating in a chaotic state. Inspectors from the Government and the casino

And now, the good news

Chaos theory often allows us to predict what a complex system is *not* going to do with considerable confidence. Chaos theory lets us identify systems that are either steady, or change so slowly that they can be safely treated as steady. Chaos theory sometimes lets us identify the possible states a complex system may reach.

regularly check each roulette wheel to make sure that the operator cannot influence the result of any roll, and that the results over a period are statistically random. Maintaining a roulette wheel involves ensuring that the bearings are running smoothly, that all the projections are perfectly regular, and that the wheel is set dead level in a heavy and stable table. In a simple mechanical system, these would be the exact actions recommended to make a machine perform in a regular, predictable way.

A cloud in the sky provides an example of deterministic chaos. Every cloud is simply a mixture of water and air, substances that can be studied in the laboratory until all their physical properties have been determined with extraordinary accuracy. Yet since the first cloud appeared in the sky above a primitive earth no two clouds have looked or behaved identically. The effort put into chaos research has paid off with advances and new insights into many fields.

Endnotes

1   Galileo, Newton and Leibnitz flourished between 1600 and 1730, and between them invented the laws of motion and the mathematics of the calculus, which enable motion to be studied scientifically.

2   A measure of Newton's staggering genius is that he did not fall for the clockwork explanation. He saw that the orbits of the planets were not quite perfect, and thought that God might be called upon to adjust them from time to time to prevent a catastrophe. Many scientists today would regard this view as naïve, but no one knows why or even whether the solar system is stable. Perhaps it is just breaking up very slowly

3   Lord Palmerston (1784-1865, Prime Minister 1855-65) was sent as a youth to Edinburgh for three years to study political economy under Professor Dugald Stewart. He became a free market and free trade enthusiast, and used the Royal Navy freely to bring others to his point of view.

4   Becquerel discovered radioactivity, Roentgen discovered X-rays, and Einstein discovered the Theory of Relativity. Becquerel and Roentgen showed that the universe did not run like clockwork, while Einstein showed that clocks don't work "like clockwork" anyway.

10. Some Mathematics of Chaos

A system property

CHAOS IS A PROPERTY of systems, not of single objects. The systems must be active and in many cases dissipative, that is, there must be a substantial amount of energy available and in many cases it is thermodynamically degraded by passing through the system. The term system implies definite interconnections between the various system components such that if any pair of components is isolated (clamped, in the terminology used by circuit designers) a forced change to one will have a measurable effect on the other: the system can be described by a set of partial differential equations.

To qualify as a system a set of related objects and phenomena must have some tendency to remain coherent without collapsing. In a mechanical system there must be both repulsive and attractive forces between its components. In other kinds of system such as electrical circuits and chemical reactions there must be analogous effects. Two principle roads to chaos have been identified:

- most iterated equations, of which the best known is the Logistic equation (10.2), will demonstrate chaotic behaviour under particular circumstances, and in some cases under all circumstances;
- *continuous* systems defined by at least three linearly independent variables of state will definitely demonstrate chaotic behaviour under some circumstances, typically under some levels of energy flow.

The first of these routes is referred to as the *period doubling* route while the second is described by a *strange attractor*. The history of a system may be plotted on a phase diagram in as many dimensions as there are linearly independent variables of state. Its initial state will be represented by a point in this phase space, and its subsequent behaviour represented by a line through phase space. When repeated trials are made, with the initial state of the system represented by different points in phase space, the different trajectories will show a tendency to converge. This tendency merely expresses the coherence property mentioned above.

Attractors can usefully be looked for at zero (for a stable system), a non-zero point (for a steady state), a closed loop (for an oscillatory system) and at infinity (for an exploding system). A single system may have several attractors, representing the ends of different trajectories starting from different initial points. Lorenz discovered a phase trajectory (found by plotting just three variables against each other) which he called a "strange attractor" because it traversed an infinite path within a finite region of phase space. Lorenz discovered the strange attractor in attempting to develop a weather forecasting model. The "butterfly" picture in Figure 3.1 illustrates Lorenz's (and mathematics') first strange attractor. Lorenz was using the set of equations (10.1)[1] as a highly simplified model of a part of the atmosphere:

$$\frac{dx}{dt} = -\sigma(x - y)$$

$$\frac{dy}{dt} = rx - xz - y$$

$$\frac{dz}{dt} = xy - bz \qquad (10.1)$$

where: $\sigma = 10$; $r = 28$; $b = \dfrac{8}{3}$

Lorenz was using a computer that was slow even for the 1960s and discovered that restarting the computer with four decimal places of data when it was working internally to a higher level of accuracy sent the calculation off in a completely different direction. The "butterfly effect", the suggestion that a butterfly flapping its wings in the Amazon jungle could start a chain of events leading to a hurricane in New York, arose both from the exquisite sensitivity demonstrated by Lorenz's equations and the suggestive shape of the diagram.

The period doubling route to chaos is found in a difference equation. May's logistic map is a result of a repeatedly iterating the difference equation:

$$x_{t+1} = rx_t(1 - x) \qquad (10.2)$$

For values of r between 0 and 1, the solution will rapidly converge on zero for any value of x_0 between 0 and 1. As r is raised to values between 1 and three, the solution will converge on:

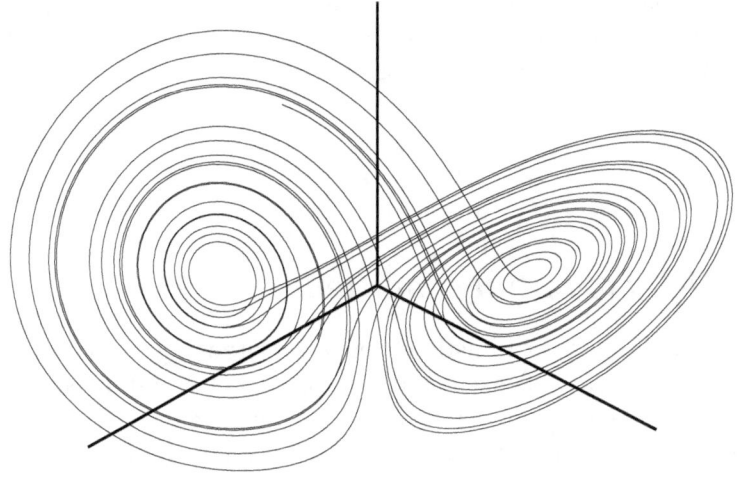

Figure 10.2 Lorenz's strange attractor in 3D

This projection looks a little less like a butterfly, but may give an impression of how the attractor twists in space.

$$x_\infty = 1 - \frac{1}{r} \tag{10.3}$$

As r is raised above 3, for any values of x_0 other than that given by (10.3) the solution will no longer converge. For values slightly greater than 3 it will oscillate between two values, and then at a little over 3.45 the oscillation will divide so that x will cycle through four values. A little higher still, and x will cycle through eight and then sixteen values. At about 3.57 x will set off on a tour that never appears to repeat itself. This is the chaotic state. The chaotic state will continue as r is raised until suddenly chaos vanishes and x starts following a three value cycle, then six, and then chaos returns.

Feigenbaum proved that every finite integer would appear as a period before r reached 4. For all values of r above 4 and x_0 not given *exactly* by (10.3), the system will take a number of values between 0 and 1 before it reaches a value above 1, then below zero on the following cycle, and thence rapidly towards minus infinity. This is a simple example of the general phenomenon of period doubling. Feigenbaum proved that a very large class of iterative systems of the form given by (10.4), that is, systems when the state at a given time is wholly or partly determined by its state at some previous time, would show identical behaviour to that shown by the Logistic Equation:

$$x_{t+1} = f(x_t)$$ (10.4)

Sensitivity to initial conditions

The hallmark of deterministic chaos is sensitivity to initial conditions: although the result of each iteration of (10.2) or future state of the system described by (10.1) is absolutely determined by the current values *of the relevant variables*, after a few iterations in the chaotic region the result will no longer be predictable. This is because a small error in the value of either r or x_n will increase with every iteration. The value of a solution to Lorenz's equations at time t depends on the value of the state variables at some earlier time t_0. For some value of t not much larger than t_0 the effect of the inevitable error in determining t_0 will dominate the estimate.

Mere mortals as well as mathematicians can discover chaotic behaviour in very simple formulae. A personal computer with a spreadsheet programme can be used to develop examples of chaotic behaviour. In Figure 10.2 the two lines represent the result of repeatedly iterating the logistic equation (10.2). To develop Figure 10.2 r in the Logistic formula was set to 3.78. A 0.1 per cent uncertainty in the initial estimate makes the result quite different by the twenty fifth iteration.

Figure 10.2 is a useful indication of the most important difference between *random* and *chaotic* systems. In random systems, all predictions are invalid, while in chaotic systems *short* term predictions may be made with great accuracy. In a chaotic system it is the medium and long term prediction task that is impossible. Clearly, any useful investigation into the applicability of dynamic systems theory to economics and business management must put some measure on the words "short", "medium" and "long". If the economy and the major markets within it responded on a time scale of years or decades, the classical equilibrium economics would have something useful to say. In fact, many critical components on an economy respond in months, days, or even minutes and most

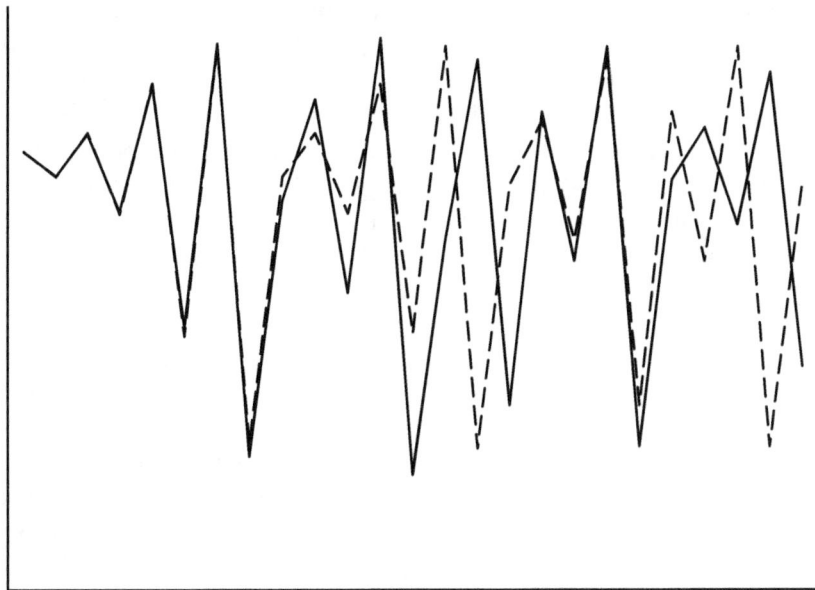

Figure 10.3 Chaos: Sensitivity to initial conditions

The two lines start off only 0.1% apart: by the twenty fifth iteration they
are moving quite independently.

predictions on a time scale longer than a few months are no better than
mixtures of wishful thinking and guesswork.

The birth of the logistic map

May was led to the logistic formula by studying the seasonal changes in
insect populations in particular ecological niches. If, in one season, there
are very few insects, they will all find plenty of food and survive to mate
and lay eggs. The next season there will be more insects, and eventually
the population grows to the point that there is considerable pressure on
the food supply. Most insects do not survive to lay eggs under such
conditions, and the following season there are relatively few insects
born. Looked at over a number of successive seasons, insect populations
may show all four system states. If for some reason the insects lay very
few fertile eggs each, the population in each successive season falls until
the species becomes extinct in that niche.

F inal stability has been achieved.

At rather higher levels of fertility, the population settles down to a constant level, with the numbers of insects in each season similar to the number in the previous season. At higher levels of fertility still, the population starts to oscillate: high one season, low the next, then returning to roughly where it started. As the fertility of the insect population becomes still higher, the population oscillations become more complex, not returning to their starting point until the fourth or even the eighth season. At a slightly higher level of fertility the population continues to go up and down, but there is no longer any repeating pattern. Chaos has arrived. The final possibility is that fertility rises to the point that a season eventually comes when so many eggs hatch that the food supply is exhausted before any insects survive to lay viable eggs. A population explosion has occurred, and the species achieves final stability with a bang, rather than a last flutter.

By constructing appropriate interpretations for r and x, and a suitable mapping of each to some real world property, models can be constructed which produce output just as confusing and arbitrary as real world data. Modern mathematical tests can be applied to real world data and in many cases they show that apparently random behaviour is really a case of deterministic chaos. The results of investigations involving the logistic equation are interesting to marketing theorists because of the strong evidence that similar equations reflect the behaviour of developing markets. In the marketing literature the equation usually appears in its continuous, integrated form. It still reflects the fact of feedback as a common phenomenon in marketing.

Fractal geometry

For a century or so, mathematicians have been aware of some families of very strange curves and shapes. Shapes such as a square or a circle were considered normal. The sides of such a shape had a definite length, and the shape enclosed a definite area. Normal shapes had been studied for well over two thousand years. According to the rules of classical geometry, geometry was the study of *points, lines, surfaces* and *volumes*. A point had position, but no dimensions. A line had one dimension, its length.

Surfaces had two dimensions and volumes had three. Classical geometers defined rules that combined points, lines, surfaces and volumes. A straight line, for example, was the shortest distance between two points. A circle was a line that was always the same distance from a particular point. A triangle was defined by three lines.

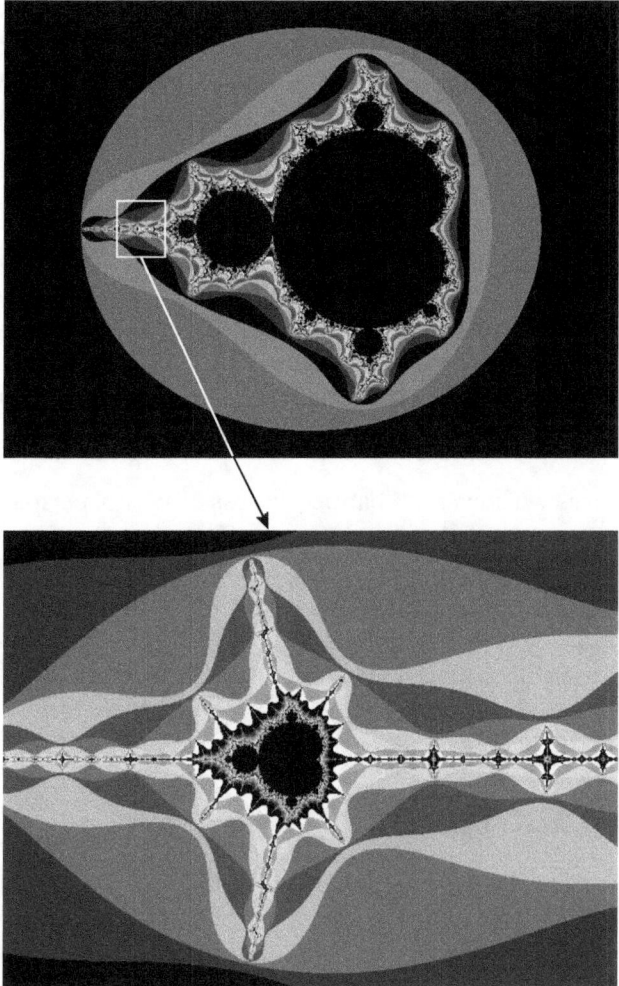

Figure 10.3 Zooming into a Mandelbrot diagram

The features of a Mandelbrot diagram are repeated at every scale; The
lower picture is a magnified view of the square in the larger one.

Source: www.fractint.org

A very minor extension of these rules was all that was needed to
create some very strange shapes. We have already met Koch's snowflake
curve (Figure 2.4). Curves such as this were originally referred to as
pathological curves. The implication of calling the curves pathological
was that there was something sick about them. In practice, the

existence of these strange curves revealed that much of conventional mathematics was sick: dying of anorexia, in fact.

Shapes that conform to the austere prescriptions of classical geometry are rare in nature, to put it mildly. Complex, involuted shapes were the rule. The mathematician Benoit Mandelbrot[2] coined the word "fractal" to describe these shapes. Once they had a name, they appeared everywhere. Real snowflakes grow in fractal shapes, as does frost on a window. The coastline of a country and the profile of a mountain range are fractal shapes. Computer games use fractal functions to generate realistic scenery. Fractal geometry is closely associated with chaos theory and was developed at the same time. Mandelbrot's eponymous curve (Figures 2.5 & 10.3) has come to be the symbol of both chaos and fractal geometry, but it is only one of a very large family of fractal figures.

In nature, whenever a chaotic process leaves a permanent result, that result seems to be a fractal shape. The chaotic pounding of the ocean on the shoreline leaves a fractal coast. Fractal geometry, and chaotic flows are also linked through the phenomenon of scale independence., A small part of a fractal picture always looks similar to the whole when it is magnified, no matter how much the magnifying power is increased. Turbulent and chaotic systems from real life also maintain their appearance under different levels of magnification.

The Polya distribution

The common normal distribution is generated by an independent set of choices. If a coin is tossed a hundred times in each trial with heads scored one and tails scored zero, the sum of the numbers recorded over a large series of trials will display a binomial distribution with a mean of fifty. When the number of tosses per trial is very large, the balanced binomial distribution may be approximated by Gauss's Normal Distribution.

When the choices in each stage of the trial are not independent the result of a series of trials is unlikely to resemble a normal or a binomial distribution. Figure 10.4 shows the result of two different approaches to a similar problem. In each case a market is assumed to be made by two identical businesses offering indistinguishable products. Each business starts off with one customer: a further ten customers arrive in the district and allocate themselves to one supplier or the other. If the new arrivals examine the two alternatives, and, finding no visible difference, they toss a coin or come to a decision in some other purely

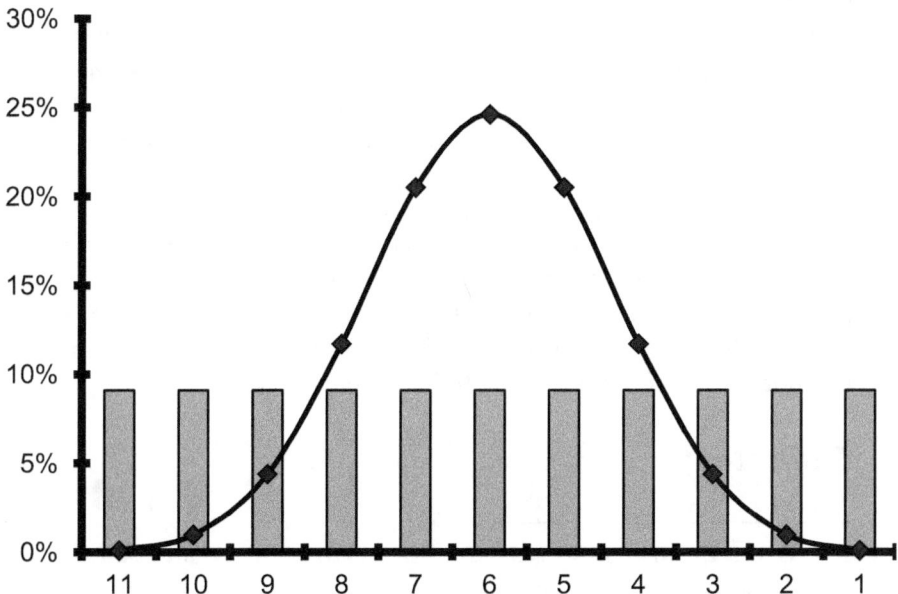

Figure 10.4 Polya and binomial distributions

The bars represent the probability of a firm having the number of customers shown on the horizontal axis when arriving customers are influenced by the number of existing customers each supplier serves; the line shows the probabilities when each arrival's choice is random.

random way the chances of one business attracting the lot are a negligible 0.1% and the most likely result is that each business winds up with between four and six customers.

If the newcomers look at their peers before deciding what to do, the first newcomer to make a choice cannot, as before, make it on any logical or visible grounds and so chooses randomly. The second newcomer, however, now sees that one business has two customers while the other has only one, and chooses the larger business with a 66 per cent probability. When all the ways that the next nine new arrivals can place their custom are analysed, every outcome is shown to be equally probable. The chance of one supplier adding all ten of the newcomers to his books is a far from negligible 9.1 per cent.

This paradox is generally ascribed to Polya,[3] who examined a theoretical game in which a number of marbles of different colours would be placed in a bag. One marble would be withdrawn, matched with one of the same colour from stock, and the two marbles replaced in the bag. Polya asked, what distribution of colours would be most likely after the process had been repeated a certain number of times?

The answer, in this case, is that *every possible combination* is equally probable!

Reverting to our two shopkeepers: there is a 73 per cent chance that one of them will wind up with at least twice as many customers as the other. It is hard to imagine that the winner in such a contest would not allow herself at least a small smile of inner satisfaction. She might get quite hurt if some reader of this book explained that she, personally, had nothing to do with the result: it was pure chance.

Endnotes

1   Stewart, Ian (1989), *Does God Play Dice: the new mathematics of chaos*, Oxford: Basil Blackwell

2   Benoit Mandelbrot, a mathematician who made significant contributions to the study and the popularisation of chaos while employed at the IBM research laboratories at Yorktown.

3   A full description of the non linear Polya problem and its solution may be found in the article by W. Brian Arthur, Yu M Ermoliev and Yu M Kaniovski (1987). "Path Dependent Processes and the Emergence of Macro Structure". *European Journal of Operational Research* **30**, pp. 294–303.